CITRINE HORIZON

A SOUL JOURNEY THROUGH HEALTH TRAUMA

HANNAH SERAPHIM

Hannah Seraphim

TSPA THE SELF PUBLISHING AGENCY, INC.

Hannah Seraphim

Citrine Horizon

TSPA The Self Publishing Agency, Inc.

First Edition

Softcover ISBN: 978-1-7778284-0-0
Electronic ISBN: 978-1-7778284-1-7

Cover Design | Ata Ojani

Book Design | Kristy Twellmann Hill
Editor | Tara McGuire

Publishing Support | TSPA The Self Publishing Agency, Inc.

the line of light as the sun rises or sets—that's
the crack of hope—the glimpse of a fresh start

PROLOGUE

I AM NOT A HYPOCHONDRIAC. Worrier, sometimes. Germaphobe, definitely. But hypochondriac? It took me a long time to understand that I was simply advocating for my health.

For many years, I felt like there was something wrong with me. I would check my symptoms with my family doctor, as often as possible without feeling like I was losing my mind. Usually, I'd get the standard response—I should get a blood test. But every time the test results came back, I'd be told I was perfectly healthy.

My doctor considered my birth control or whether I was dealing with anxiety or depression. Most of the time, I'd leave her office relieved, but not far after the appointment I'd be revisited with a strange feeling of radio static deep in my chest.

There is something wrong with me.

So when, on a typical day at my office job in corporate communications, I was chatting with the company's doctor about ways to promote health in our Vancouver office, it didn't come as a total surprise that he furrowed his brow and said, "Hannah, I don't want to alarm you, but I think it would be good if you asked your doctor for an ultrasound on your neck."

His keen eyes noticed an unusual bulge at the base of my neck while I was standing in the doorway of his office, a good two metres away. Of course, he told me not to google anything. *I googled.* He also said I shouldn't worry. *I did.*

I always felt uncomfortable with my neck. Like something was constricting it. It's not like I went about my day unable to breathe. But once in a while, I would be lost in thought or relaxing at home when I would feel a heaviness—a weight of energy like a too-tight choker around my neck.

I was born with the umbilical cord around my neck. As my mom put it, the doctor used "salad tongs" to pull my oxygen-starved blue body out of her. People describe birth and mention their baby's first breath; well, my first breath was more of a laboured gasp. Perhaps I carried that feeling with me. That memory as a newborn is something my brain couldn't recall, but my body would innately bear.

The day I spoke to the company doctor was the catalyst for my life to flow through a path only meant for me—towards my inner truth and light. This book is about the experiences of my mind, body, and soul—separate and together—through a complex and transformative health journey.

WAITING, ANTICIPATING

I'M IN A WAITING ROOM. Waiting rooms will be one of my frequent hangouts. This waiting room has been a long time coming. I had been putting off making this appointment for a while now. I've known something is wrong for a while now.

The permanent weight on my neck is getting harder to ignore.

Now that I'm here, I'm scared. I take a few deep breaths, but I don't find it helpful. Every breath feels constricted. My lungs cannot access oxygen the way I would like. The palms of my hands have a sheen of sweat.

A lady holding a clipboard calls my name. "Hannah, please follow me." I wipe the sweat from my hands onto my black leggings and stand up. My heartbeat accelerates, the dampness returns to my hands.

A tired-looking ultrasound technician with brown hair pulled up into a messy bun and wearing periwinkle scrubs is already in the room when I arrive. In a monotone voice she tells me to lie down, gesturing to the examination table. I settle in on the cold, papered surface while she squeezes a goo onto my neck, unconcerned about getting it on my grey wool knit sweater.

I could've taken it off if she had warned me. The thought is a necessary distraction as she begins to probe my neck. The goo warms up as she slides the wand side-to-side, but the pressure soon gets much worse.

I attempt to look around the room with a stretched and still neck but can only see the speckled white ceiling and the technician's puzzled face. Earlier she had the expression of someone living in the mundane all day. Something about my appointment must be shaking up her day a little bit. She frowns and pushes harder. Tears form in my eyes as I'm unable to get a breath in. I try to speak, ask for lighter pressure, but decide to stay quiet so this experience will end sooner rather than later.

my breath

the tears

wishing

hoping

knowing

this is

the start of

something

She chucks a hot towel wrapped in plastic on the side table so I can wipe the gel off my neck. "Your doctor will call you with the results," she says, and rushes out of the room, neglecting the space between her words and my questions.

My nerves are in shock. My body shakes. I'm not ready to hear the inevitable.

Finding a way out of the medical imaging centre, I again feel the wand's phantom pressure on my neck. I can't seem to get a breath in—wheezing, my pace quickens. I want to get to the car as fast as possible.

In and out, my breath is laboured. I can see the condensation producing a fog in the winter air; shivering—I notice my coat is not on me but in my hands. Turning the corner, I see my old grey Volkswagen Jetta. Running now, I reach the door handle. Traffic, car horns, construction muffles as I fling the door open, climb in, and slam it closed.

After fumbling to put the keys in the ignition, I crank up the heat and place my hands on the steering wheel. I tremble as tears pour from my eyes.

Blurred vision. I don't know what's ahead.

RING, RING

A WEEK LATER, the doctor's office calls. I must come in person to discuss the results.

YOUNG = HEALTHY?

ANOTHER WAITING ROOM. The smell of antiseptic. Clean and cool. This time, I don't have to wait long before I'm called into an examination room. Doctor Duncan, my family doctor, walks in with an empathetic look in her green eyes.

Speaking like she isn't in any rush, articulating each consonant with a certain purpose, she says, "Hannah, how are you today?"

"I'm good! How are you?" I'm impatient to hear the results.

"Oh, you know, just another busy day. All is well!"

I smile and stare.

"So, you're here to talk about your results from the neck ultrasound? Yes." She answers her own question as she starts typing on her laptop, finding my file.

It turns out they've found some nodes in my thyroid gland that look a little different. Doctor Duncan wants to refer me to an endocrinologist—a specialist that treats hormone-related diseases and conditions—to assure it's nothing serious as I'm young and healthy. The scan images seem to show I may have Hashimoto's disease, which is an autoimmune disorder.

"It's not too difficult to treat; we may just need to put you on medication to help balance your thyroid."

I see in Doctor Duncan's eyes that she feels sorry she didn't recommend an ultrasound sooner. I can't blame her for not doing so. She ordered the standard blood test check any other doctor would do. I'm young and healthy, after all.

"Okay, thank you." I smile, my eyes not hiding my worries.

THE CROW

"SWALLOW," Doctor Wagner says as he pushes his pudgy fingers down at the base of my neck. I'm at the specialist's office for the thyroid check. He presses a little too hard, and my eyes start to water. Then he leaves the room, returning with a student close to my age who looks at me as if I'm a chapter in his textbook.

Doctor Wagner's beady eyes stare at my neck while he informs me they will do a biopsy. Then and there.

"Oh, okay." He doesn't meet my eyes. The fear crawls up my spine.

When I scheduled the appointment I had no idea this was a possibility, and I lay down on the examination table in shock.

Doctor Wagner tells the student to push his fingers down on my neck in a particular spot—they're clammy. The two men look at each other and leave the room. I hear Doctor Wagner's terrible attempt to whisper in the hallway that he'll let the student try a biopsy today. I want to protest—I'm not a biology experiment. But I don't.

I can't speak up to this doctor who seems like he wants to move on to the next patient as soon as possible.

The student returns, and I tell him I'm going to close my eyes because needles make me feel faint. He nods with feigned confidence. His gelled light brown hair is unbothered by the movement, sticking straight up. I can see on his freckled face that he doesn't know what he's doing. I look at him one last time before closing my eyes, praying he'll be gentle, hoping he'll treat me like a human being and not a specimen.

His first attempt fails as Doctor Wagner hovers behind him, saying he's missing the thyroid nodule where a tissue sample needs to be extracted. He pushes the needle around under my skin, trying to find the right spot. I try to stay calm, but it feels like a metal worm is crawling under my skin.

Again, the needle is inserted. Doctor Wagner takes over to ensure he gets a good sample, pushing the needle even deeper—his hot breath on my face. I keep my eyes shut, and hold my breath until he's done. Roughly, he retracts the needle. I breathe in and feel the soreness it left. They say the biopsy is complete—relief sets in, and the tears I've been holding so carefully well up.

As the pent-up tears trickle down my face and onto my neck, Doctor Wagner decides to take one more biopsy. I hear him speaking but the words don't register. I hold my breath and try to appreciate his thoroughness as he takes the final sample.

Looking like I've offended him by crying, Doctor Wagner sticks a Band-Aid on my neck.

As he walks out the door, I hear him say, "We'll contact you about your biopsy results in three days." The student had already left the room, sometime between my tears and the Band-Aid.

In a daze, I walk to the bus that will take me home. I try to listen to each step as my feet hit the pavement. But it feels like I'm walking on a stream of fog. All I can hear is my muffled heartbeat drowning out the city sounds.

The world has stopped. I feel frozen in time. I make it to the bus stop and ride the eerie haze home, not quite remembering how I got here. Going through the motions, I unlock the front door and step inside my apartment.

Windows closed. Bare trees jostling outside in the cold winter wind. I sit in dead air. Staring at my feet. Fingers tracing the Band-Aid on my neck. I don't want to think about it, but the foreboding presence of time stings. Why is this happening? Could my health be in jeopardy at twenty-six years old?

Abrupt taps on my balcony pull me out of the trance. It's a crow. She sits on the metal railing staring at me. The thought pops into my mind—bubbling to the surface.

Cancer.

I look into her black shining eyes.

Cancer.

I plead for the thought to go away. The crow just sits there, staring. Not moving, not menacing, just all-knowing. Preparing me. Warning me. Cancer.

She flies into the late afternoon air.

the crow painted
the sunset
with her feathers
and whispered songs
from her beak

if only you knew
how delicate life is
if only you cared
to look up
and see

As the sun sets, casting light across the Spanish white walls of my living room, I take a deep breath and call Dustin, my partner of four years. Then I call my mom. Both know I was going to get examined for Hashimoto's disease today. Although I'm not ready to tell them my fears, I know they expect an update. I mention the biopsy, ensuring the test is routine—I'll receive the results in three days. Cancer is a possibility, but a tiny one. My mom asks if she can take me to the next appointment; I tell her I'll be fine.

I'll be fine.

The next three days go by in a blur. Working long hours and avoiding everything else is my modus operandi when I can't keep anxious thoughts in check. I step out of my Yaletown office building, shivering as I put on a toque over my ears, and walk to Doctor Wagner's office with my bruised neck and sunken spirit.

The sky is grey. The walk takes about twenty minutes. The rhythm of movement allows my brain to process the biopsy, the crow, and the possible results. I feel very alone, but I need to be alone right now. Vocalizing my worries could mean they come true. I'm too scared to admit my fear to anyone.

When I arrive outside Doctor Wagner's office, as much as my mind fights it, I feel the message from the omniscient crow in my body, whispering the truth in my soul.

how did you take it in

the news.

did it slip
into your eardrums

hit the bottom
of your stomach

did it float into
your chest

create static

did your lips quiver
lungs pause

did you feel numb
legs jelly

did your soul astral project
above your body

to the point of no return

check all of the above.

THE NEWS

CANCER. Thyroid Cancer. Papillary Thyroid Cancer. Thyroid Cancer. Cancer.

I leave Doctor Wagner's office—one foot in front of the other. I walk along the cracks in the sidewalk, staring down, unaware of anyone or anything. All I know is I must move forward. Turning the corner to cross the street, I realize my parents will want to know, so I call my mom. The phone rings, and as I reach the other side of the crosswalk, she answers.

"Mom, I don't want you to worry because I'll be okay, but I didn't get the best news from the specialist. I have thyroid cancer."

I can hear her breathe on the line, opening her mouth to speak.

Before she has a chance, I fill the space by saying, "Apparently, it's the best cancer you can get."

False laughter reverberates into thin breath escaping my lips. I try to sound calm when my body is in shock while it holds confusion and despair.

My mom asks if she can give me a ride home, saying I shouldn't go back to work after hearing this news. I take her advice but tell her I'll see if Dustin will pick me up instead. *He's the only one who can comfort me right now.* She understands and says she'll let my dad—who I also work with—know, relieving the burden of telling the news to anyone further. Ending the call, I say that even though the word "cancer" sounds scary, I will be alright.

I try to believe what I'm saying.

I call Dustin. His linear algebra class at Simon Fraser University finishes around now. I ask if he can come downtown before going home.

He says yes and then asks about the appointment, and I blurt out, "I have thyroid cancer."

As the words leave my lips, I realize how insensitive I'm being.

He fumbles with his words, "W-what?"

I don't have to see him to know he's shaking.

I tell him I will be okay and I'll see him soon—his voice cracks as we say goodbye.

I wait in the coffee shop nearby, sitting in a daze so thick I can almost see the fog surrounding me, suffocating me. To calm down, I think about how I fell in love with Dustin when our eyes locked from across the room at a mutual friend's birthday party and smiled like we were in on the same joke without uttering any words. Ever since that moment, it's been easy to express what's on my mind, heart, and soul with him.

Why did I tell him over the phone like that? Why did I say this news so nonchalantly? I wish I had been more gentle. I don't want to make a big deal about it, but how is he supposed to take cancer as not a big deal. I've prepared myself for bad health news. But I haven't shared those thoughts with anyone other than the crow that came to my balcony.

Dustin pulls up to the curb in front of the coffee shop in his dark blue Volkswagen Jetta, and I run to the car door. We look at each other, knowing nothing said right now will make either of us feel better. He leans in for a quick kiss before flicking the turn signal to merge back into traffic.

I scan his profile as we drive over the Lions Gate Bridge. His knuckles are white from squeezing the steering wheel too hard—the speckled gray in his dark brown hair, his clenched jaw. He blinks behind his glasses as tears escape his chestnut brown eyes. I realize I haven't cried yet as I reach to hold his hand. I'm numb—he feels *for* me.

EMOTION AVALANCHE

WHEN WE GET BACK TO MY APARTMENT on the North Shore, Dustin and I don't know what to say. We sit in silence, holding each other. I don't ever want to let go. Numb and exhausted, we watch a movie and eat dinner. He goes home and I fall into bed.

Alone, the only thought I can hold onto is, *I don't ever want to let go.*

The following morning I wake up feeling like I'm still dreaming. I listen to the voicemails my parents and brother have left saying I'm strong and that they love me. It's hard to listen to. Hearing their love and the sadness in their voices, knowing I can't make them feel better. In my dad's voicemail, he says I don't have to worry about going to work today, he's told my manager and she understands. At least I can be relieved about that.

My mom, brother, and his girlfriend visit me for lunch. We sit at my kitchen table drinking our smoothies. I feel their need to be here as much as I need them to be here. Even though I am wired to hide away and be in my thoughts, I need them here so I won't dwell on the news I can't change. My brother Greg breaks the silence to ask me how I am.

"I'm doing okay. I just feel really tired." That statement is true. I feel okay because I feel nothing. My eyelids are heavy. I'm exhausted.

They stay for the rest of the afternoon. We play card games and laugh. When Dustin is off school, he comes over too. Dustin plans to stay over this weekend even though I know he has a lot to study for a big test coming up. I'm grateful he knows I need him right now without having to ask. My mom leaves and then soon after, my brother and his girlfriend do too.

Dustin and I are now alone. I can tell he doesn't want to think about anything either. His eyes look tired, as if he hasn't slept. We decide to play Scrabble and watch a movie to avoid the passing of time and the saying of six-letter words that begin with C.

a loud guttural noise
coming from somewhere.

she didn't move. candlelight. a half-finished
game of Scrabble on the coffee table. her boyfriend
sleeping on the couch.

she stares into the sound, the dark reflection
of the window. blinking. a wetness
runs down her cheeks.

peak crescendo. her boyfriend
snaps out of his slumber—almost
falling off the couch.

"Hannah I love you," pain
in his eyes—the wailing
sounds are coming from her.

shaking uncontrollably, she brings
her hands to her cheeks—wiping
away tears. but she can't stop.

tumbling to the ground—
avalanche of emotions.
she touches the cold floor.

he pulls her up.
holding her. consoling
her—frozen in shock.

yesterday I learned.
I have cancer.

ILL-FATED PREMONITION

THE NUMBNESS OF SAD NEWS SHATTERED. The truth has reached my soul. I think about all of the possible health outcomes. I think about all of the ones I love. The thoughts roll around—an infinite loop of grief and fear.

Every day, I worry I am a burden, that my health has brought stress to those I love, which affects their health, which in return affects mine. Every day, I look at Dustin, the one I love the most in this world, and I wonder if I should leave him to save him from me.

howling
wind through
vocal cords

tears turn
to rain
body melts

to earth

human or
saltwater
soil
air

WHAT IS REGULAR LIFE?

TIME PASSES, and I'm learning to live with the diagnosis and what it could mean. I return to everyday life while feeling completely irregular. Wake up, work, go home, sleep. I go through the motions so I can't disappoint the person I'm supposed to be or foil others' expectations of me. The illusion is quite successful. At least from my perspective, no one can see that my feathers are ruffled. I like it that way.

I keep cancer a secret, only sharing when I have to. With brief moments of vulnerability, I take myself out of my avoidance routine to share the news with select family and friends. Sometimes I receive so much love, and other times, pity. Or worse, no empathy at all. Or even more dreadful, too many tears; I don't know how to console others when I haven't learned how to soothe myself.

I build an invisible shield around my heart so people can't see how emotionally frail I'm becoming.

I hold the news close to my chest. The shame is locked in my neck. I wonder when I'll ever take a full breath.

I know why
the secret is kept
cloaked words uttered
lift reality
shaping new projections

all will change
future too close
conditions too heavy

if this secret
is told
not a single
soul
will look at me
the same

the me I am
will be
forgotten
turned, twisted

broken

burdening those
who practice sympathy
if the secret is revealed

I'll never see
myself the same.

FRIENDS

I HOST A MONTHLY KNITTING NIGHT with some friends. Most of the time, we don't really knit but instead, chat and drink wine. Knitting is just a quirky excuse to get together. Although, I've been working on a scarf for the past three months—rectangles are pretty easy unless I've drunk too much wine.

It's been two weeks since the cancer diagnosis, and I'm ready to tell these friends who I consider to be confidants.

"I have some not-so-great news I need to share with you."

I see all eyes on me; my palms are sweaty. I take a sip of cheap red wine, feeling a shudder in my chest.

"You know how I sometimes complain about my hormones and energy levels? Well, there's a reason for that. I went to a thyroid specialist, and it turns out I have thyroid cancer. But apparently, it's the best kind of cancer you can have."

I gulp down a chunk of air.

My friends stare, and I can tell they don't know what to say. One fidgets with her napkin while saying she's "glad it's nothing serious."

The other asks, "Oh, does that mean we can't have knitting nights anymore?"

A burning sensation reaches my core. I'm appalled, but I don't want them to see my pain.

"Yeah, I'm sorry. I don't think I'll have time to host while I'm busy dealing with all this health stuff."

Backing off, she looks down at the ground and says, "I understand." But does she?

they say, "that kills me"
slap their knees and laugh
"I almost died"
when a shameful story is told.
each time these words
meet my ears,
my heart
falls into my
stomach.
it's hard to hear that language
when death feels like
it's resting on my shoulders.
a clinging friend
that knocks on my temples
reminding me of mortality.
I wonder if one day I'll think
of death more trivially.

The next day, I'm still in awe. I didn't get the responses I hoped for or expected with these friends. I think of the nights I've comforted them through heartbreak or listened to them vent for hours about not being treated well in their jobs. They didn't offer that same support in return.

I'm the friend that is the support system, the one to lean on. Maybe I inserted myself there.

back facing
I lean into
outstretched limbs
that can't hold

me

falling through
veiled whispers
convincing
I'm not good enough
to be held

for I am the holder
I stand like a mountain
heads rest
on my shoulders

people leave
the boulders
when the rocks slide

CALL OF THE VOID

TONIGHT, I'M COOKING DINNER. Chopping the veggies for our stir fry, I slice into a node of broccoli, watching as the branches break off, the green buds clinging to their appendages.

Hoping the cancerous tumour inside me hasn't spread, I try to ignore the thought that continues to visit at night. But, I cannot—holding the knife, the unwelcome fascination creeps in. The knife's weight, cool to the touch. The sharp blade shimmers.

echoes
reverberate

cut it out
cut it out
cut it out

pick up
the sharpest knife
slice

the tumour

cut it out
cut it out
cut it out

I listen
\   /
\ /
\/

I forgive myself for dwelling on these thoughts. I'm easing my way closer to the idea of my mortality as I cope with daily life. I realize I don't want the "regular" life I've created. I can't pinpoint it exactly, but nothing I'm doing feels right anymore.

Cancer is revealing the bubble I've put myself inside, and popping it in the process. I can't see outside of what I'm living through now, which feels broken and abandoned. I've been walking through life without really feeling alive.

CANCER IS NOT ME

I STARE IN THE MIRROR AND SWALLOW—watching the slightly round bulge on the left side of my neck roll up then down.

My fingertips press against the skin of my warm neck, leaving red blotches in their wake. How did I not notice it before? I've been ignoring my body for so long, expecting it to function. I never thought to check my neck. No one ever told me to. I'm learning it's not up to others. Only I know my body and it's time to get reacquainted with it.

With every specialist appointment, doctors with cold, clammy fingers prodded my neck and asked me to swallow. A simple check to see if my thyroid gland is enlarged. It's so visible to my naked eye, it all seems obvious now. If I focus on the lump for too long, I can feel it every time I swallow. With each breath I take, my lungs expand a little shallower. My chest is heavy and my airway more constricted.

I can't wait to have the tumour cut out and I hope the cancer hasn't spread. Part of me wants to fill all this anxiety and emptiness with love, and part of me fuels the hostile feelings until I'm completely undone.

I never thought I would have to prepare for something like this, but who does? The mental toll of merely connecting the word cancer to my own body is unbearable. Cancer is not me but it is in me. I cannot escape it.

At the same time, a deep knowing is pushing up to the surface trying to tell me this is meant to be. I must not be angry or scared—I must face this experience to allow my soul to follow its predestined path. I try to trust these thoughts because my other ones are much darker.

At least this quiet voice is telling me I'll be okay.

Cancer,
you're dead to me.
I am so much alive

the spirit in my bones
arms rise with sun
ocean waves—hope love joy

can't you see
feet on earth

26

don't you know
I need years
to give live enjoy

I dream
toes in soil
praise sky
jump
into moon water

laugh into light
upon edges of clouds

wildflowers frolic
campfires dance

everlasting burn
deep being
eager days
no meaning

You must die.

LINE OF LIGHT

MY FAMILY TAKES DUSTIN AND ME TO DISNEYLAND. They want to cheer me up. I try to cheer them up too. I can't help but think this is their way of spending time with me, *while they still can.*

eyes light up
childlike wonder

too many churros
all the rides

fearless

because there's
more to

fear
at home

fireworks fly
eyelids dim

Tinkerbell's wand
blesses the sky

make a wish

The family trip shows me I can still be full of life and laughter. It's okay to be in the moment and forget the rest. Separating myself from cancer is necessary to survive—I'm allowed to not carry my grief all the time.

Lighthearted, Dustin and I continue on to the Grand Canyon. A place I've wanted to visit since forever. We rent a car and drive from Los Angeles through the bustling, dense neighbourhoods into the barren desert. Cacti sparsely poking up into the never-ending horizon. My mind transitions with the scenery. The city is complicated, like my need to always be busy—to avoid the grief I feel. Here I sense the airiness of the desert validating the flow between grief and joy.

"I'm enjoying this road trip," I say, one arm hanging out the window.

Dustin turns down the song "Hurricane (Goldroom Remix)" by MS MR from his curated playlist—he always makes the best ones for our trips.

"Yeah, this is exactly what we need right now." With one hand on the wheel, he reaches over to squeeze my thigh.

I smile. "It really is."

A blur of beige, burnt umber, red rust, sage, and dark green meets our eyes before we begin to ascend into a pine tree forest. Fine sand sifts off our car as fresh sharp wind welcomes us. We have arrived.

Jaws chattering, we throw on sweatshirts and run to the edge of the canyon; too excited to delay the experience any longer, we'll check in to our hotel after. The sun has just disappeared behind the ridge of the western canyon, and we witness a bright yellowy-orange line over the rocky cliffs, holding a citrine glow.

Embraced by the canyon walls, the light dips along my neck before it flows into my soul and ignites my being. I've never felt more alive than I do right now—this sunset is one-of-a-kind. My feet are held by the Redwall Limestone, but I feel like I'm floating. Exhilaration moves up my spine and into my heart.

I'm here. I'm alive. I'm here. I'm alive.

I'll leave my fate to the citrine light as it holds me in balance with the stars, the moon, the earth and the sky.

touch neck
close eyes
paint light
golden hues
in mind

power always
inside
promise
to foster
citrine light

VIEWPOINTS

IT DOESN'T TAKE LONG TO STRAY from the here-and-now mindset I had adopted at the Grand Canyon. Back home reminiscing about the trip, I'm putting away little mementos I collected, and I feel a deep sadness. I'm longing for my life before cancer where I felt invincible and could see years span out to decades and all the new memories I'd collect.

It's in my nature to be future-minded; I plan goals and daydream about my next adventure. Now, the future scares me, the past saddens me, and the present pains me.

Undressing, I tell Dustin to soak in my essence. I ask him to hold me, to take a photo of my youth and scarless neck. To take in all that I am now. I feel like I'm on the precipice of losing myself.

jaded by
my own haunts
beliefs
toted alongside

slip
    into
        my
            lungs
            arduous
        in
    and
out

fitful energy
in my chest
steals time
creeps up
my neck

stiff jawed
belfry rings

can't rip myself
out of this one
no escape
or asylum

go through
the haunted corridor
change this fate

meet mind
and body
exchanging
the onus
for axiom
until soul
speaks out

set me free

Most days I wake up with fear in my chest. That life is not forever. Each day I force the reminder that these fears may propel me into an extraordinary life. A more genuine life I can no longer take for granted. Where the present will be even sweeter than imagining the future. Maybe the way I view life needs to change. I'm recalibrating.

MOM'S MEMOS

MY MOM TAKES ME to every appointment—notebook in hand. Furiously writing what the doctor says. Word for word. As the doctor speaks, I hold on to every comment—clasping onto hope and faith. Diagnosis to prognosis to surgery to treatment to recovery. Five phases with a thousand steps in between.

I listen, thyroid pounding in my neck, producing a storm in my head.

The clouds evaporate the words that just reached my ears as I step out of the antiseptic-smelling hospital and into the fresh air to head home.

My mom goes to her house, types out her notes and emails them to me. As I read through the details of prescribed diets and doses, I feel overwhelmed.

Thyroid throbbing, mental cloud returning.

And so, the days move on between doctor's appointments and regular life. Detail upon detail, I forget time and due dates. I sleep in and get to work late. I worry about socializing, I forget to socialize. All I can do is try to survive—the bare minimum kind of life.

My mom becomes my memory, recording and scheduling what's important. I forget the rest.

I couldn't remember:

the appointments

and medications

and diet

and next steps

I couldn't hold it all in my head because:

the fear

the shame

the grief

were making a home in there instead

DEPRESSED HURRICANE

DUSTIN AND I ARE SITTING ON THE COUCH. I'm wrapped up in a fluffy blanket with extra layers of grief and despair. I'm breaking my own heart as I tell myself I should leave him. I can see the suffering in his eyes, the hopelessness, the unrequited love he has for a body that's empty.

My soul left a long time ago. It lives somewhere above my head. The past two months have chipped away at everything I thought I was and everything I am.

I'm grieving who I was, who I am, who I may be.

Dustin doesn't see it. He doesn't detect the daily storm consuming me as I plan for my death—the end. He sees me as everything I've always been. He believes in me and our love. He believes in the health and immortality of my body. It's just another day where I'm half-heartedly giving him an out to save him from me.

On other days, the sun bursts through the clouds, bringing hope. We lie together entwined in so much love I almost forget my soul isn't present. I want to give him all of me, all my love—smothering before I go.

I'm a depressed hurricane, an unpredictable weather pattern, swirling and thrashing love at him and just as quickly taking it away.

pain in your eyes
suffocated emotions
held under
you're calm
to make me feel better

how do you see me?

avoiding gaze
to not show
never know

carry the pain
take it away
so I can feel comfort

but I want to see
anguish
within
the angles
of your face

walk my fingertips
along the surface
to know I'm
not alone

you smile
in the empty space
cry in the provoking

is this my end?

I'll love you in
every moment
of every day

you free me
I grow and burn

you love me
selflessly

I wish I could
give you more of me

etch my skin onto yours
permanently

CUT IT OUT

the doctor appointments

the unknowns

"it isn't like it's life or death"

but I won't know until they

cut open my neck

"it's not life or death"

but people have died

from the very thing

my body is fighting

"is it life or death"

The clock ticks by in the surgery waiting room as I sit on a stiff plastic taupe chair in my baby blue surgery gown, hair net, and socks. My body tries to ignore my mind's mental labyrinth of anticipating whatever is coming next.

With clenched fists and a stiff jaw, I try to crack a joke to show calmness to my parents, who plan to stay at the hospital during the surgery.

"I was worried my butt would be hanging out of this thing." I point to the gown. "Glad it wraps all the way around!" I grin.

My mom laughs.

My dad chuckles. "That seat sure would feel cold if that was the case!"

"And sticky!" I smile with a grimace as I shift my bottom from left to right, hearing the chair squeak.

We all smile and laugh for maybe a little too long—avoiding the next space where we breathe in and remember why we're all here.

At two o'clock in the afternoon, a stocky woman in scrubs that match my gown comes out to let me know I'll need to wait a while longer. The surgeon, Doctor Hamilton, is tied up doing emergency surgery.

My mom's concerned voice says, "You must be so hungry. I'm sorry you have to wait longer, Sweetheart."

I haven't eaten since last night, but my nerves satiate me, feeding at my anxiety and sweat-tipped fingers.

"I actually don't feel hungry at all."

I walk out into the hallway and call Dustin. He's at school about to write an exam. It's like the Universe wants to make sure the layers of stress today go deep. I wish him good luck as he does for me. We're both heading for unfamiliar territory. Neither of us knows what the outcome will be. We leave the call with "I love yous," an ache in our voices we try to ignore.

Just as I begin to toy with the escapist notion the surgery might get cancelled, I hear my name. Once "Hannah" hits the open air of the waiting room, time moves quickly and I feel like I'm moving slowly. Rushing to say "love yous" to my parents, I hug them, looking past the strain in their eyes, and gather myself to walk towards the operating room.

I squint under the too-bright light. I try to acknowledge the sea of blue scrubs. There are at least five people, including Doctor Hamilton, in the room. Everyone is moving around like worker bees with a cordial melody of laughs and pleasant commentary. I assume they're trying to make me comfortable, but the smell of disinfectant, the tray of surgical utensils beside the bed, and the stars in my eyes grip at my anxiety.

Doctor Hamilton has been a welcome relief these last couple of months. He's compassionate and confident, two attributes that have brought some ease to this whole process. But, even as he says hello with his booming voice, I stare at his large hands, trying to see if they look steady and hoping he isn't tired after the emergency surgery earlier today.

Doctor Hamilton asks about the family trip to Disneyland, and I respond, but in an instant, I can't remember what I said. Everything around me seems to be moving quicker than I can follow. I start to believe I live in a different mode while the rest of the world moves ahead—a dissociated alternate reality. I don't want to be left behind.

In my time-lapse, they've ushered me to the surgical bed, lying there as the anesthesiologist tries to find my vein. Talk swirls around and I smile, trying to say an equal amount of pleasant words—feigning a casual air while I hold my breath. My heartbeat pulls at my chest.

Now, as if time snaps forward again, the anesthesiologist puts the oxygen mask over my nose and mouth to begin her countdown. I take the deepest breath I have all day and tell myself *everything is going to be okay. Everything is going to b…*

I wake.

up from
deep sleep
completely unaware
sweet moment
of forgetting
no need to feel
just exist
before the pain
creeps in
remembering confronts
the mind
although it's scary

I'm alive.

strapped in
gone under
hours and hours
awake
numbness moves
up from
feet into legs
from hands into arms

is this body mine?

sore
swallowing hurts
dry mouth
aching back
muscles don't move
for fear of
tearing the stitches
in my neck

My parents and Dustin come in to see me. They say the surgery took three hours longer than expected, but it went well. I can see the fear and sleep in their eyes. I can talk, but it hurts. A knife lodges in my throat.

My parents leave me with Dustin while they do a quick run for food. They tell me it's past eight o'clock and they haven't had anything to eat since lunch. I swallow sharpness and can't imagine wanting to eat food ever again.

Dustin stands at the end of the bed, and I notice the look of shock in his eyes, although he's trying his best to hide it. Staring at my bloody, bandaged neck, he turns pale and falters backward. My brain can't comprehend what's happening. In a moment, nurses steady him and bring a chair. They help him down as he puts his head between his legs. They get him a lollipop and juice. If I could cry, I would, but it hurts too much.

I don't know what I look like, but I'm not ready to see. A slice across the neck can't be appealing. All I know is the longer I'm awake, the more I'm in pain.

The post-op nurses rotate their patient checks. At least I think it's more than one nurse. All I notice is a blur of faceless bodies buzzing around the room. They come by often to ask what my pain level is. I always say six not to sound too weak but also not too tough because it really hurts. Every time I tell them my pain number, they press a button beside the bed. I'm not sure what it does.

Dustin and I smile at each other as he enjoys his lollipop and I savour the feeling of floating.

My parents come back, and my mom says she will stay in my hospital room overnight. I'm relieved I won't be alone. Dustin and my dad say their goodbyes and go home to bed.

bloody gown
sways with
the
f l o a t i n g

pain blocker
lollipops
we're
f o l d i n g

spaces
between
choke the
k n o w i n g

I stay in the after-care surgery room for a while longer until an exhausted-looking nurse with scraggly grey hair rolls over a hospital bed, saying it's time to be moved to the room I'll be staying in for one night. As I try to lift my body out of the surgery bed, everything begins to spin. The nurse decides she'll do the bed switch when I'm already in the new room.

Up we go in the elevator. I keep my eyes closed the entire time. We arrive in a dark shared space with the gentle snores of other patients. While I'm still spinning, she tells me to lift my body and move onto the new bed. Raising my upper body and getting onto my elbows brings a deep pain into my neck. I can't seem to use my muscles. Everything feels heavy. I cry out as I try with all my might.

Moving from one bed to the other is the hardest thing I've ever done. The nurse shoves me a little bit so I'm not hanging off the side of the new bed. My mom gently nudges my legs over so I can shuffle onto the middle of the mattress.

Without warning, because I've been feeling nauseous this entire time, I begin to throw up. The nurse rolls her eyes and mutters something about too much morphine. She's not interested in dealing with a difficult patient and walks out of the room. My mom grabs paper towel from the washroom and does her best to clean up.

A little while later, I realize I have to pee. I tell my mom and she gets the cranky nurse who walks over with a bedpan. After throwing up, I'm not as nauseous but the pain is worse. My mom and the nurse help lift my bottom as the nurse scoots the bedpan under me. Whimpering, I pee on myself.

My body doesn't feel like it's mine.

FATED

THE NEXT MORNING, I'M STILL REELING from the morphine, but haven't been able to sleep. My groggy mind and body get startled when a new nurse comes into the room to take my blood. He's sassy and friendly. I can't respond to his quick-witted humour, but I appreciate it. I'm thankful the nurse from last night must have finished her shift.

Blonde bangs dishevelled, my mom sits up from her makeshift cot against the wall to get out of the way for the nurse. I can tell she's uncomfortable after sleeping with her bad back on a lumpy surface, but she continues to put on a brave face.

A little later, after I've reluctantly eaten two spoonfuls of orange-flavoured jello for breakfast—barely swallowing so the slippery gelatin coats the sharpness in my throat—Doctor Hamilton ambles in to give us an extensive update now that I'm a bit more alert. With a big smile, he says the surgery went well; it just took five hours to get it all. The tumour was so large they had to remove my entire thyroid. Cancer had also spread to lymph nodes on my vocal cord and down the left side of my chest, but he believes he got it all through the one incision across the base of my neck. He says I must have had cancer in my body for at least six years.

His words sink into my scarred neck. My mind is validated for all the years of worry that something was wrong in my body.

As he walks past the hospital curtain and out of view, I thank him, with a hoarse voice, for doing everything he could to help me.

My mom looks depleted. "I'm so upset we didn't know about this sooner. Are you okay?"

"I am. I actually think it's fate."

Her eyes widen. I can tell my words sting. I continue to speak.

"I think it stems from being born with the umbilical cord around my neck. I've always been sensitive there. You know how I get. If someone tries to touch my neck, I recoil, perspire, and even get a prickly feeling inching up my spine. It all kind of makes sense now."

She looks down, "Oh."

Feeling like she's starting to blame herself for my suffocating umbilical cord birth, I decide not to tell her my other revelations, like how I think the sensitivity to my neck affected other parts of my life. My voice needs a break anyway.

born.
blue skinned
gasping for

air.

umbilical cord
wrapped
around neck

cut off
but
never left.

ghost cord
invisible vine

clinging shadow.

till tumour
sliced out
of neck

...

first true
breath

NUMB

DESPITE MY NECK FEELING VERY SORE and the muscles in my body staying clenched, what I'm more scared of is the numbness and tingling in my legs, arms, and lips. Blood tests occur three times a day because my calcium levels aren't returning. It seems as though the parathyroid glands that help balance calcium in my body were damaged as well.

shy veins
parched
blood drought

scudded
skin dam

doomed arms
harpooned

pray
purple patches
heal

A day goes by, then three. I still feel like I'm in slow motion, imagining I move like a slug or a turtle. I see the wishful glint in the nurses' eyes, wanting me to heal quicker so they can move me out of the room. No one wants to overstay their welcome.

The nurses have resorted to crushing up calcium pills and putting them in applesauce—a chalky mushy concoction to go down my swollen throat. I'm taking about seven calcium pills a day and the numbness and tingling seem to be lessening.

On the fourth day, I can walk from one end of the hall to the other without taking any breaks. My newfound strength seems to be a sign that I'm ready to go home, even though when I sit on hard surfaces, like a toilet, my legs go numb almost immediately.

HOME EMBRYONICALLY

I STRUGGLE TO WASH. I can't reach my arms up above my head. I can't get my neck wet. My mom helps me climb onto the kitchen counter with a stepladder. My entire body is in pain. It's hard to remember that only my neck was operated on.

After my mom moves all the thoughtful "get well soon" cards and flowers from friends and family, I lie down on the counter, and she gently holds my head over the sink. She pours shampoo in her palm and carefully threads her fingers through my matted hair. I wince, unable to keep my head up without feeling a heavy deep pain in my neck travelling down my body. She wraps my head in a warm towel and helps me down off the counter. I move like I'm sixty years older.

I'm led to the bathroom and strip down, climb into the bathtub. She uses a cup and cloth with soap on it. I scrub as best I can. She rinses me off with warm water from the cup, then swaddles me in a towel. I feel like a caterpillar, cocooned and cared for, despite the pain. Clean, after all the time spent in a dirty hospital, where I walked around in socks with unidentifiable hair on the floor. Being home, feeling clean, and being loved by my mom, is all I need right now.

After a few days, I step into the shower. Making sure the bandage is protecting my neck. I lather up and rinse off. I slowly clean my hair and body. I feel independent—more in control of this body, even though I still feel empty.

As the days progress, we create a consistent routine. Every morning I wake up at the same time to take my pill, and then I lie in bed on a mountain of pillows to prop my neck up until breakfast, which is about an hour later. I must not eat before that. My mom makes oatmeal and then proceeds to crush the calcium pills in a coffee bean grinder, mixing them in applesauce. After breakfast, I try to walk around my apartment. My entire body aches, but after being strapped down for a five-hour surgery in an awkward position, my muscles and ligaments need to readjust. Life before this didn't feel so calculated. Over small increments of time, I'm learning to enjoy the sense of control I have.

My throat and neck feel swollen, and when I try to speak, my voice cracks. As much as I mentally prepared myself for surgery and recovery, I don't think even the doctors saw this coming. No one said I might lose a part of my voice, that the pain would reach all corners of my body, that my limbs would go numb, and my lips would tingle because my body can't keep up to absorbing the calcium it needs. Most told me I'm young, that I'll bounce back, that I can go back to work after two weeks, but my body seems to have other plans.

In the afternoon or evenings, Dustin visits for a while, and sometimes my mom drives back to her place or goes grocery shopping so we can have some time to ourselves. I miss him more and more when he leaves.

My dad comes over many nights to eat dinner with my mom and me and watch *Schitt's Creek*. He buzzes and always says, "Roland Schitt!"—pretending he's one of the eccentric characters on the show. I always laugh, appreciating the humour he wants to bring to my day even before he steps through my apartment doors.

My family and Dustin do everything they can to provide pleasant relief, keeping my mind off the pain. I still can't tell if it's the physical or emotional pain that hurts worse.

bedridden.
tired. sore. sick.

I can't go far
but I think about
how I travel with the sun.

I think about
when I'll sing again—
the birds sing for me now.

I think about
hands held,
laughter escaping my lips
watching those I love—
cheer for their
vibrant lives.

I think about
how I'm still here—
still breathing.

kept alive by this
tiny pill.

every day I take
a short trip
with the sun
as I go for a walk
around my kitchen island.

After the operation, my parents started telling their friends that I had thyroid cancer surgery, and I also let a few more friends know—too exhausted to hide from my reality. I receive an outpouring of cards, flowers, and gifts. I'm groggy and overwhelmed but thankful for those sending love.

My parents are great gatekeepers, asking those who send gifts to bring them to their house instead of mine. They'll then deliver the thoughtful items to me themselves. Right now, I don't want visitors. The thought of allowing others to see my weak, damaged body is paralyzing. I don't want others to see me like this. It's not how I want to see myself.

The first week, I make an exception for my friend Hayley to visit. We've been friends since we were twelve years old. We like to think we bonded on our own terms, but really it was our moms who talked us into being friends when we were both shy pre-teens.

My mom opens my front door for Hayley and she walks in, bringing a card and a beautiful purple orchid.

Before she can see me, she yells, "Hello, Lola!"

That's the nickname she gave me in high school.

"Hey, Hayley!" I say as my voice cracks.

As she turns the corner and notices me, I can see on her face how alarming I must look. My uncombed hair is in a messy ponytail, there's a bandage on my neck, and my pajama-clad body is stiff from my head to my toes. I wish I could hug her, but I'm too sore.

Hayley expresses her concern and asks me how I'm feeling. All in a tone that shows that she accepts me for who I am right now. I don't have to fumble along, finding words in the conversation to make her feel comfortable with me like I've felt inclined to with others. We can just be. I realize having Hayley see me like this is worth it to get to see her.

Sometimes you need your close friends. Sometimes you need to crack open to let the love in.

After four days in the hospital and two weeks recovering at home, it's time for my mom to leave my side. This blip in my life feels like it's all I know. Eighteen all-consuming days, a fragile reality I cling to because I'm scared to see what else life may bring. Tears well up in my eyes because I know it's time to say goodbye to the makeshift shelter my mom cannot sustain. I don't think I'll ever know how to express and show her how much her time here means. She fed me every meal and made sure I took my pills. We shared stories and laughter; we cried and just sat together.

I'm sad because it may be the last time we ever get this sense of closeness. At the same time, I know I've been living in a fantasy world. I'm in a warped comfort zone like I'm her young child again. To truly heal, I need to go through the rest of this healing journey on my own.

sometimes I just want
to be held by my mom
listen to her heartbeat
soak in her wisdom
and strength
she'll stroke my hair
kiss my cheeks
I'll close my eyes
where hopeful deep blue
filled them

my eyes are now
empty—
placid

in my mother's arms
I make a wish
to feel again—
like me again
and for a tender moment
I believe it will work

but as we release
the protective embrace
holding me together
maternal—
strong as the light of a full moon
I remember consoling
will not make me whole

healing isn't linear—
it's lunar
a churn of phases
a journey only I can take
as I bare my soul
asking it to reflect in my eyes
to bring the blue back
the wild back
my life back

~~||||||~~

IT'S TIME TO SEE MY NAKED SCAR. I had a slight peek at it in the hospital when they took the gauze pad off and replaced it with Steri-Strips, seeing my reflection in the dark window beside the bed. But now we're about to get up close and personal. The once white strips are beginning to peel off, greying and curling over like the pages of an old notebook exposed to the sun and rain. Wishing they'd hold on for a bit longer, I grab the first strip that's slightly overlapping the other one, with shaky fingertips and hold my breath.

It comes off with ease, and I breathe out before removing the last layer that's unable to hide the faint horizontal line, a slight ridge under my skin from the dissolvable stitches.

I tug carefully at the corner of the Steri-Strip, feeling a shooting pain—I've barely touched my neck. I stop for a moment and gather myself before peeling it off, so slowly it takes at least two minutes—prolonging the full scar reveal. As each new millimetre exposes more of the incision, breath gets caught in my chest, my eyes water. While my fingertips remove the last of the bandage, I close my eyes, recollecting my scarless neck, the beauty of my youth. Reminding myself I'll be okay, and I can get through this, I raise my head and look at my reflection.

Besides the swelling and dried blood that makes me quiver, I can see Doctor Hamilton's precise cut along where a neck crease already existed. I tell myself this is the best-case scenario. It's quite thin and shorter than I thought it would be, considering they took out my entire thyroid and additional lymph nodes. Although I'm pleasantly surprised with the incision, I still feel queasy looking at it for too long. I leave the bathroom, adhesive residue still sticking to my neck.

A few days later, I must start massaging the stitches in my neck with a little bit of soap when I'm in the shower to make it easier for them to dissolve. I try to touch the spot where Doctor Hamilton made the incision. My hands shake, and my breath gets heavy—fingertips skimming my neck, the invisible stitches under my skin, tiny markings, bumpy and jagged. I exhale and noise escapes my mouth.

the scar	no love here	loss lives	forever severs
foreign object	discomfort	in mind	invincibility
quarantined	pricking wound	body denies	fantasy

Doctor Hamilton said eventually my body will absorb the stitches. After much time, perhaps years, the scar will be unnoticeable. Even if that's true, it's hard to believe I'll ever not feel scarred and fragile.

my scar is a crater

like a big rock chipped
off a mountain

but craters over time
can hold water
plants and minerals

the sun and the moon
always find
the crater

maybe I'll find my element
in this emptiness

too

+++++

marked territory
cross
if you
dare

barbed wire
comeback trail

sky
borders
sea

follow opening

INVISIBLE

I EXIST IN A LIMINAL SPACE. Chained to a weak, healing body and the person I was before cancer, while my twenty-six-year-old curated identity desires freedom and robust health.

On the outside, it probably looks like I'm living a pretty ordinary life. Now that my mom has left, I go grocery shopping and cook myself food. I go for walks and meet up with friends for short visits. Dustin sleeps over on the weekends. I'm still not working. I'm not ready yet.

But on the inside, so much is changing. I can't keep track of who I am anymore. My body, mind, and spirit are defective. I can't see myself.

Every day, my body murmurs that I need to heal. I can't run into life without it running into me. When my mom stayed with me, I would walk around my apartment. If I did a full lap, I would be proud of myself. The pain from surgery had crept into all my muscles and tightened them.

Now I go for walks around the block. I hide my scar behind a bandana or turtleneck sweater. Some days, when I cross the street, an impatient driver honks, signalling I should walk faster. In those moments, I try my best to give them grace and give myself the same in return. They can't see I'm walking as fast as my body will take me and I can't see why they are in a rush. We all have our silent struggles.

My pain is invisible, and it's not just physical.

cotton swathed neck
patterned bandana

wrap wrap wrap

take away
painful reminders
curiosities
judgments

wrap wrap wrap

hiding
my scar and
what I can't face

trusty square fabric
emotional bandage
lifeline to hide
scar line
stepping out
but hidden
shrouded in secrets
held close to
my neck

wrap wrap wrap

Today, my friend Ata texted to say he's baked peanut butter cookies and would like to drop them off. He has a knack for checking in when I'm feeling alone while also not asking for a big-time commitment. Ata is the first friend I ever made on my own in pre-school when we were both four years old. We have a connection that exists within unsaid words, philosophical conversation, and silly dancing. He's a friend I find it hard to isolate myself from, and I'm glad he doesn't let me do that.

He comes over and I reveal my scar to him.

"I'm Ms. Frankenstein over here," I laugh.

"I can't even see the stitches! They did such a good job."

"Yeah, I'm quite impressed. I still feel like I'm scary-looking to people, but it isn't that bad."

"You aren't. You look great," he says with honest steadiness to his eyes.

I smile, giving him an appreciative look as I chew a delicious peanut butter cookie.

I'm not invisible to everyone.

THE IN-BETWEEN

THE TREES OUTSIDE ARE BUDDING just as I begin to feel more like myself. But now, it's time to prepare for radioactive iodine treatment. I must go off the thyroid medication and start a low-iodine diet to get my body ready. In a month, I will be receiving a dose of Iodine-131 to kill any remaining cancer cells.

The thyroid medication helped me feel better. It replaced my lemon-of-a-thyroid with a slice of hope. The first few days off the medication were fine, but after a week goes by, and then two, my body aches for relief. I'm always cold, my muscles are weak, my memory deteriorates, and I'm nauseous.

I'm feeling an unfamiliar emptiness. I'm a shell trying to be whole again. Inescapable anxiety is etched onto my breath. In and out, in and out. Please escape these queasy lips. Please let time move a little faster.

This is the in-between. Maybe I feel extra sick because I'm scared. I'm scared of going through treatment and the doctors telling me I still have cancer. I'm scared the treatment will affect me in the long run. Iodine-131 is the same ingredient that was released into the air after the Chernobyl disaster. It's hard to wrap my mind around that.

I remind myself that sometimes it's necessary to go backward in order to go forward. I'm holding on to that slice of hope.

My brother Greg is taking me out today to help pick out a keyboard. I feel terrible, but I'm excited to spend time with him. I slowly get ready—trying to sing along to "Higher" by Rihanna playing on my phone as I comb my hair in the bathroom. My voice cracks and I feel an instant pang of sadness. I used to sing higher notes, and I wonder if I'll ever get my voice back to the way it was. I remind myself that at least I can talk. It could've been much worse.

Greg calls to say he's outside to pick me up. Grabbing my trusty bandana, I tie it around my neck. Then, taking a can of ginger ale out of the fridge, I put it in my purse. I can't manage car rides without drinking something bubbly these days. Nausea hits unexpectedly, and I don't want to ruin this time with my brother.

We drive into the city. With slow sips of ginger ale and Greg making me laugh, I feel a little better. His dry sense of humour reminds me of how we both learned to mask our emotions growing up by using sarcasm. Mastering words instead of feelings used to keep life light. It doesn't work the same way for me anymore.

Arriving at the music shop, we walk through, and my fingers trace along the keys of the first piano I see. A peculiar buzz moves from my fingertips into my heart. I feel nostalgia wrapped in freedom—a sense of being alive.

I loved playing the piano as a child—learning the songs and the satisfying feeling of my fingers remembering the notes as I sang along to the lyrics. Why did I let that part of me go? Why did I forget the melodic happiness of learning a new song? With the keys hitting my fingertips and the sounds hitting my soul. We test out a few pianos and pick one out on the spot. I can't wait to bring it home and play again. I can't wait to feel free.

looking through
cancer lens
not sick
more sentient

physical
vs.
soul

fails

for destiny
requires the
chorus
in one breath

FRIENDSHIP GEMSTONE

A FEW WEEKS BEFORE MY TREATMENT DATE, Emily calls. She's one of my closest friends—we attended high school and university together.

"Hey, Hannah!"

I'm excited to hear her voice as she lives two provinces away and sometimes it's hard to catch each other for a phone chat.

"I have something to tell you," she shares.

"Oh!?" My eyes widen as I listen to her say, "I'm coming to Vancouver next week!"

An energetic buzz runs through my nauseous body, adrenaline taking over.

I scream, "Ahh! I'm so excited. Are you coming to visit your family?"

"Well, yes, I'll be seeing my family too, but the reason I'm coming is to see you! Can I sleep over one night?"

When Emily arrives, I'm elated. I have a few close friends who don't live in Vancouver, and it's been hard reaching out not knowing how to ask for support. Phone calls are nice, but basking in the same energy of someone you love is so much better.

Emily and I spend the weekend laughing so hard I find it hard to catch my breath. We talk all night; I almost lose my voice. But, caught breath and lost vocals feel pleasant this time around.

As we reminisce on the years of memories we have together, my memory lands on the time we travelled Europe in the summer of 2011. I close my eyes, thinking of how freely we lived, how life felt carefree. Then, we move on to talking about how our trip ended.

I had a mysterious allergic reaction and was given pills by hospital staff in Florence, Italy, which helped tame my swollen tongue but also broke down my stomach lining. Stomach lining breaking down isn't pleasant, and as we moved on from Florence to Cinque Terre, my condition worsened. Emily found me on the linoleum hostel floor writhing in pain, clutching my stomach and vomiting.

After yelling at the hostel staff, who would not call an ambulance for a good fifteen minutes, Emily finally persuaded them, and we were taken to the closest hospital about an hour away in La Spezia. She stayed with me all night while I laid in a cot in a general waiting area, surrounded by other ill and injured people who had not yet been helped. She stayed with me when I was released from the hospital but could still not walk very far—finding a hotel nearby to recuperate. She ventured out onto the Italian cobblestone streets to find rice and green tea for every meal—as the doctor ordered—and watched Italian MTV with me even though we had no idea what the reality stars were saying.

Emily, who is now a professional nurse, nursed me back to health. I feel so fortunate I was one of her first patients.

That was the last time I had a health scare until my thyroid cancer diagnosis. Emily is always there for me.

Emily asks, "Where do you think you want to travel to next?"

I smile in adoration for my friend who sees me for me. She knows travelling is one of my true loves. I've explored all around North America, Europe, and Southeast Asia. It's been my goal ever since I was twelve years old to set foot on each of the seven continents. I tell her I think I want to go to Australia and New Zealand next. It's nice to be reminded of the dreams that live within me, the ones that exist outside of the wish to be cancer-free.

On the last night of her visit, my family invites Emily's family over for dinner. Clinking glasses and happy conversation is the proper send-off for Emily to go back to Saskatchewan and for me to get ready for the isolating treatment.

We hug each other goodbye extra tightly—as though we're pressurizing our friendship and memories into a precious gemstone.

LIMITS

THE DAYS GROW WARMER AND LONGER. Winter is in the rearview but I still feel cold. The treatment date was supposed to be today, but the Iodine-131 drink hasn't arrived at the hospital yet. I need to wait a few more days until it can happen. I'm agitated.

The past week has been challenging. I feel off, not being on my medication, and still learning to live in this thyroid-less body. Nausea, muscle aches, and memory lapses are only worse now.

For the fifth time today, I scan the instruction sheet I received from Doctor Wagner. He told me that if the treatment doesn't work the first time, I'll have to do it again. That's intimidating, as all the preparation leading up to now has already been quite daunting.

Besides no medication, the low-iodine diet has been difficult. Iodine helps make thyroid hormones, and for my treatment to work, any remaining thyroid cells need to be starved of iodine so they fully absorb the radioactive iodine treatment and are destroyed.

There's an extensive list of what I can't eat, including fish, dairy, or anything with iodized salt. Iodine seems to be a star element in many foods. I've resorted to baking my own bread, straining and blending my own nut milk, amongst other culinary adventures and mishaps. Half the time, I don't feel like eating anyway because of the nausea.

The sheet outlines that I'll need to isolate myself for one week at home and all the surfaces I touch with my skin will need to be cleaned and disinfected—radioactive residue will seep out of my pores and bodily fluids.

Then come the risks. Most sound minor: fatigue, nausea, dryness and a metallic taste in the mouth. Although, after doing my own research, I know there are also chances of fertility loss and developing other cancers. I hope the treatment will do what it needs to do and overlook me for any extra destruction it could cause.

After posting the instruction sheet back on my fridge with magnets, I busy myself while I live within these limits—cleaning to put my mind at ease. I wipe down all the surfaces and put away items to reduce touchpoints. Then, I organize the magazines, colouring books, and novels I've received from friends and family on the coffee table. Having my apartment ready makes me feel ready. Despite my nerves, I'm also excited to be on the next and, hopefully, final step of ensuring no more cancer lives in my body.

RADIOACTIVE

TODAY IS FINALLY THE DAY. I am at the hospital sitting in the nuclear medicine unit's waiting room with my mom. We've been waiting for a while, and the appointment time has passed by about half an hour. I go up to the front desk to see what's going on. It turns out the vital ingredient I need for the treatment is still in transit.

In disbelief, my nauseous body goes weak and I try to respond to the nice lady at the desk as if I'm totally fine with waiting longer in this stale void. I wobble back to my chair where my mom, who's heard the whole conversation, asks me to help her with a crossword. I entertain her request as I see she's trying her best to preoccupy my anxious mind.

Two hours after the scheduled appointment my name is called. Eagerness to get the treatment over with calms my nerves. Ten steps from the waiting room, I walk into a fancy-looking chemistry lab. I watch as staff move around wearing head-to-toe protective clothing. Their gear looks like the same rubbery material as the x-ray bib you'd wear at the dentist, but thinner. I'm wearing jeans and a sweater.

A woman walks over—her protective gown swishing towards me. She's clasping the Iodine-131 treatment in her gloved hands. At arm's-length, she offers me the radioactive iodine in a weird-looking canister with a straw sticking out of it. I sip on the drink and almost chuckle. It seems comical that the treatment is in a bizarre sort of pop can, as though I ordered sparkling water at a café.

I finish the clear, flavourless drink, and the woman takes the container with her rubber gloves and then gives me a card to note the treatment I had and a timestamp for how long I may have radioactive traces in my body—it will be several months. I had read that if I went to the airport, I'd set off the body scanners and found that absurd, but now the technician warns me, I'll need to bring this card with me if I plan to travel within the radioactive time period. *Fun, airport staff may mistake me for a bomb.*

Within ten minutes, I'm on my way out the door. Keeping distance from my mom, I sit in the back seat of her car while she takes me home—worrying I'm too close.

As my mom pulls up outside my place, it hits me that I won't see any other human beings for several days. Air kisses goodbye; I race from the front door of the building to my apartment, careful not to touch anything with my bare hands, thankful the hallway is empty.

I lock the door and take a deep breath.

I record myself bobbing my head to "Radioactive" by Imagine Dragons using a funny filter that makes my hair pink and eyes look extra large. I send it off to my parents, Dustin, Greg, Hayley, Ata, Emily, and a few more friends and family who are worried about me.

As the day goes on, I start to feel terrible. I lie on my couch and feel the first wave of sickness take hold. The nausea I had experienced before the treatment feels easy by comparison. I tell myself I will get through this—I will be okay.

slave to this body
Universe fragment
anxious
uncertain
no one to

console me

hold me
within
questioning

hoping
grasping
tainted touch

radioactive residue
radiates
lime green light
surrounds
penetrates insides
pores ooze

power brink
alien creature
in/consequential
superhuman

DREAM DAYS

I had dreams—
weird dreams.
felt like summer break.

a lackadaisical wave
of consciousness.
precordial catches.
lost elucidation.
heat and dew drops.

the never-ending ending
to foundation.
finding nothing
then everything.
returning it for
Ring Pops and Fudgesicles.

forget to put the shades down.
the sun hits the skyline.
days fleeting into dreams,
dreams befitting days.

tumid peaches lull the tongue.
sweet and sour—
nature's neurosis.

tie dye died.
friendship bracelets unravelled.
cradled in the sun's clasp,

benumbed crystal void.
rescued by the ocean's tenacity,
drowning in its life-giving shimmer.

seasick or just sick.
I'll be better soon.
in the meantime,
you can find me here.
I had days—
weird days.

In my dreams, I see a glowing green orb that turns pink. It enters the top of my head and wiggles its way down my body. The colours morph between nurturing and love as the light filters through my space, aura, being.

"Heal," I plead. "Heal me."

Fitful energy and madness vibrate through every nerve. I'm living in visions and dreaming in hope.

I exist in the painting
hanging in my kitchen

the brushed pathway leads
to the forest
cool air runs down my back

from the sweep of the branches
I'm in the painting
on my wall

moss and mushrooms
grow up my neck
linking to the trees
feeding the soil

I live in the painting
because I can't live out there

outside my window,
there's an off-white sickly
plastic bag stuck in a tree

I feel sad it's not free

Katy Perry's "Firework"
plays in my head.
wishing for it to fly,
catch the next gust
to an unknown destination.

on a windy day,
it fills with air and
for a fleeting moment,
I think it will break free.

but it never does.

it's stuck in that tree,
too high for anyone to release.
I wonder if anyone else
watches from their window.

I lie in my bed,
watch the sun
east to west,
reflecting light and shadows
through a dirty,
ripped plastic bag,
and try to feel a gust
of wind
below my feet
to carry my ailing body
and vibrant mind away...

OUT-OF-BODY

FROM THE DAY I LEARNED I HAVE CANCER, I have been picking at the connection between my inner being and body. After surgery and treatment, I realize how disconnected I am.

My spirit decided to move out a long time ago. Spirit looks down at frazzled Mind and broken Body, wondering if it will ever want to return.

I'm a crab who has lost her shell. Tender and insecure, shy to go out into the world, scared to be exposed to society's critical lens.

I'd much rather live above my head.

when body failed, mind

coped

by disconnecting

health from who.

live in the stars instead. chart

the meaning

from the Universe

leaving body behind

to fend for itself.

I forget to love myself. In this body, in this world. I love the space above my head—between this world and the Universe. I live in the sky, reading the stars, receiving the energy from outside of myself, and forgetting I need to be here. The more I ignore my flesh and blood, the emptier I become. Loving this vessel could one day mean Spirit will come home, but Mind isn't ready to admit that detaching from Body is the wrong way to survive. I've been ignoring the part of myself that needs to be loved the most.

YOU CAN GO

I SLIP THE PRESCRIBED ANXIETY PILL under my tongue. Ironically, I'm nervous because I've never taken medication like this before, but it dissolves as quickly as my irrational thought. In a couple of hours, I'll be lying in a narrow tube. An MRI machine will scan my body for an entire hour to see if any traces of cancer are left.

I know I will feel claustrophobic, so I made a relaxing playlist a few days ago in preparation. I hope Bon Iver, Feist, The Japanese House, Daughter, and Vanessa Carlton will get me through.

When I arrive, three MRI technicians say hello and appear to be in great moods. I want to be cheerful for them too. I'm scared, sweaty, and can't tell if the medication I took earlier is helping. My heartbeat is fast as I lie down on the cot, and the peppiest of technicians slides me into the machine. Leaning over my head, I see her navy blue scrubs above as she sets up the music.

Then it begins. "Holocene" by Bon Iver plays. His voice in my ears, "Someway, baby, it's a part of me, apart from me..." Closing my eyes, I imagine an oscillating pink and green light surrounding me. All the healing and love I can envision swirls around this body that's had cancer for at least six years. I'm so focused; I forget where I am. When the technician comes by to say the scan is done, I'm perplexed. I thought I'd be more claustrophobic—itching to get out. But now it's over, and not only did I manage okay, I feel at peace. Maybe the medication worked, but I think the meditation worked more.

All three technicians look at me and smile. I smile back, not sure what to do or what to say. The peppy one tells me the scans came back clean.

Clean.

"Oh," I say, "that's great."

I don't know what clean means.

"You have no cancer in your body. It's the cleanest scan we've seen in ages!"

I freeze. My heart drops to the bottom of my stomach. I breathe. I stare. My mind starts moving again, soaking in the words still hanging in the air.

"Thank you," I smile, but other than that, I'm not listening to what they're saying, to what I'm saying. I think I say something along the lines of, "Wow...what am I supposed to do now?"

"Nothing, you can go!"

I can go.

I can go...live my regular life now?

It's as if I'm back in the moment I was told I had cancer. I'm moving within a bubble. Voices sound far off, and my feet don't feel like they're touching the ground. I levitate out of the room, into the hospital's hallway, where my mom is waiting with wide eyes, wanting to hear what happened.

"I'm cancer-free," I say, overwhelmed, forcing a smile.

Her face brightens, skipping over to squeeze me real tight. She says something about how happy she is and that I must feel great. I call Dustin, and he answers right away, just as shocked as me, but relieved. We didn't expect to hear the results on the spot.

My mom texts my dad and brother. I text a few of my close friends to let them know. My dad calls me, overjoyed.

I'm done. I'm free. It's over.

I DON'T FEEL FREE

I DON'T WANT PEOPLE TO LOOK AT ME DIFFERENTLY. I don't want to be seen as weak, someone to feel sorry for, so I keep my struggles in a tight-knit corner, barely sharing with those I love.

I tell myself it's because I don't want to burden anyone.

People call me strong. They say I did well dealing with this situation. I guess that's the feedback you get when you hide everything from everyone.

If only I had shared the torment inside my head earlier. If only I could admit that I don't feel strong. I want to move past the moment just like everyone else, but life isn't that simple. Healing journeys aren't simple. I'm still isolating myself.

Now that I'm cancer-free, it's easy to see how fast others want to have the experience behind them too. I allow them to move on by not telling them I haven't. I enable them to be worry-free because I pretend I'm carefree.

This mentality is trapped in the pain I have not expressed. I'm constricting my own breath. Again.

why must I forget

to move on? will
forgetting help in some
way?

I try. "move on
it's over."

I try. as mind
tells body,
hold:
the pain
the grief

I wish I could escape.

the rest of them do—
out of sight out of mind.

I am cancer-free.
but not free.
I don't think
I ever will be.

the cancer is gone,
but I'm still healing.

body grimaces, mind
withdraws.
I tell everyone I'm
okay, but I'm not.

I'm better. not better.

I don't know how
to tell them.

I need help. life will never
feel regular. I'll never
be the same.

medication sucks.
limbs go numb.

mind hasn't wrapped
around what happened.

I'm.   still.   in.   it.

OCEAN SECRETS

MY MOM TAKES ME ON A SHORT TRIP to Vancouver Island. It's been three weeks since my treatment, and two weeks since learning I'm cancer-free. Being on a regular diet and getting back on the thyroid medication has improved most symptoms, but I'm still waiting for its full effects to kick in.

Most days, I've been cooped up at home, waiting for time to do its job and heal me. I'm excited to escape the humdrum for a new environment. Even though the nausea is pulling hard on my spirit, especially after the ferry ride, I'm ready to do some exploring.

We arrive at our little log cabin, and it looks like the tide is fully covering the shore. I stand on the deck and close my eyes, breathing in the salty sea air. The ocean feels so close I could touch it. There's wisdom in my breath; it stays in tune with the waves as they lap up to meet me. I'm calm, and I'm whole.

I want to remember this moment. I'm constantly feeling pushed and prodded, nauseous and unwanted, but I can always meet myself where the sea joins the sky to feel whole again.

The following day we get up early and go for a walk along the rippled golden sand. The tide is far out now. It will take ages to make it to the ocean. I take off my sandals and press my feet into the smooth, wet sand—nature's reflexology.

As we walk, I notice all the little creatures living below my feet. Tiny crabs scuttle along the rippled sand as I imagine how I'd trek along rolling dunes. I spot a silvery-white sand dollar, and the beauty in its death astounds me. Its spirit is long gone, body hardened from the sun and air, preserving its intricate markings before the skeleton slips away into the sand. I lean down and gently touch its polished, smooth surface. The ocean whips at my hair, the scent of salt lingers in my nose.

I feel the beginnings of a tender thread, as delicate as the sand dollar's skeleton, weaving together my mind, body, and soul. I hope one day I'll be in tune with the power of nature and the tides of life.

I'll hold the ocean
in my hair
as it whispers
secrets from its depths
salt-slicked stories
from times recounted
centuries ago and
moments ahead
steeped into the same words

WHAT DID YOU DO TO GET CANCER?

I BEGIN TO OPEN UP to those who seem curious. I try, with quivering lips, to say aloud, "I had thyroid cancer but I'm now cancer-free."

Many people embrace me, "That's such great news!"

But I also receive questions, or rather, statements, that are hard to take in. As though getting cancer was my fault.

"You're so young. Did you live a healthy lifestyle?" "Did you drink too much or smoke?" "Don't you exercise?" "Do you eat well?"

If only it were easy to answer these questions. As if the answers could somehow reveal a loophole to avoiding cancer altogether.

I got thyroid cancer, and now I'm cancer-free. The mystery before, during, and after—the hows and whys and shoulds and coulds, will never be solved. If they could be, my doctors would've told me.

I sometimes think the probing from others is so they can find answers to save themselves from future suffering—by learning about my own.

here I am again
over explaining
filling in gaps

questions upon questions

I barely remember
the people who ask
but their curiosity
crosses the border
of insensitivity

so, I create a spiel
to avoid the ache
inside my chest
say it over and over
until I stop losing my breath

palms sweat
nerve endings ignite
give them all the same words
guard my mind

I watch their faces
search for the right words

to respond

maybe they shouldn't
have asked
I apologize for them
overcompensate to
help them through

I guess I made them
uncomfortable
before they made me
uncomfortable too

how are you.
how am I?
do you really want to know?

I've been cut open
and stitched up
I've taken a dose
of a radioactive substance
no healthy person would endure
I held the hands of those
who could not handle it
I've been held by those
that would hide their pain
because
I'm the problem
I'm a nuisance
I've ruined plans
and troubled minds
I've left some festering
on their own mortality
a harsh reminder
either forgotten
or burdened
left trying to explain
the unexplainable
I've lost a piece of me
to gain a part of me
a jewel within

I had cancer.
now I'm cancer-free.
so, how am I?
I'm fine.

I'M NOT FINE

I GATHER BODY AND SPIRIT and put them in separate boxes so they can't collude against Mind. I tell them to do as I say, for it's time now to get back to reality. They poke and prod at their boxes, whispering questions I do not want to hear. *What reality do you hope to return to? What is regular life for you? What's the life you want to live now?*

And with the last question, I seal the lid over the words and the feelings and move forward. That's what I'm supposed to do. It's expected of me, or maybe that's what I've learned to expect of myself. And in some ways, it's easier to go back to the life I've always known than to listen to my body and spirit asking me to dive into uncharted waters.

I walk into work. I feel eyes prying. Not only am I going back to work, but I receive a temporary promotion to fill in for a maternity leave. I hope to feel excited about this, but instead it feels like a burden. The old me before all this was excited, but the titles don't seem to stroke my ego like they used to.

After work, I rush home for my private workout session with my friend Catrina. She's just received her personal training education and is giving me special treatment by doing sessions at my home. I'm not ready to go to the gym where people can see how weak I am. Catrina's seen and heard my struggles these past few months, and I really appreciate her support to help get my body back to strength.

She walks me through a set of low-impact exercises, focusing on watching my body to make sure I'm moving my muscles properly.

"Hannah, are you breathing?"

I look up at her, coming out of my squat and gulping air.

"Don't forget to breathe," she gently scolds, then demonstrates how I should be breathing during a workout.

The breathing exercises make me feel uncomfortable. I don't know why.

After she leaves, I sink into my couch, thinking about how many years I've trapped my breath.

Catrina showed me how the simple act of thoughtful breathing is one of the greatest forms of love I can send to my body. I'm not sure if I'm ready for that yet.

Days go on, and I dive headfirst into work, cancelling personal training sessions and social plans. In the heat of summer, I have to work every day due to a crisis. I throw myself into the high-pressure situation as if my life depended on it. I'm trying to prove I'm strong even though no one is watching. No one will ask me if I'm okay if all I do is prove I am capable of the extra responsibility and will drop everything to be available for them.

I take media calls, assist the executive team with news releases, create employee crisis plans with a coffee in my hand and a smile on my face. But despite my workhorse demeanour, I'm not okay—I'm just resorting to who I was before cancer. A Type A kind of autopilot.

Meanwhile, the thyroid medication is still finding balance in my body while I ignore the stiffness climbing up my neck. I avoid the whispers telling me to question my purpose, asking why I am doing all this.

It takes thirty-one straight days of work before my body loses the adrenaline it's been living off, forgetting to replenish my life force, my soul. The mental and physical exhaustion I experience results in a sinus cold and days of migraines.

Body screams at me to reconnect to it—crying out for ignoring it for so long, for going through the motions, for not loving it. Mind catches up just as Body begins to recover from the cold, telling me I'm doing nothing right and I can't move forward. Shaking me hard, paralyzing Spirit. I can't do this anymore.

heart broke. it laid down
on the floor of stomach. making it hard
for lungs to expand. "there's no room
for you here,"
it flopped and prodded at organs.

"I don't see the reason to move home,"
heart told me. "life is different now.
no love, sadness, or anger. I feel
nothing at all."

"what can I do to make you feel again?"
I asked heart, pleading for her
to go back to normal,
pulse throbbing at neck.

"I may never feel the same again
but if you love me, if you
take the smallest steps
to love yourself again, maybe I'll feel better."

but I wasn't ready. so, I stayed
in the same spot on my couch.
as the past six days, letting
heart break
a little bit more.

I'm petrified of wasting my life, but I can't seem to move forward. I do not know why I'm still scared. I've been holding fear inside my body for a long time while simultaneously learning to let go of what happened to me.

But fear is a stronger companion.

Fear feeds on all the attributes I hold dear, traits I learned to display my entire life, replacing them with demons. The parts of me that want to self-sabotage. Fear does not care about what I've been through or what I've overcome. Fear tells me every day I will die even though I've been told I will live. Fear tells me I will lose everyone I love. That it's better to be alone, to not share this with anyone. To hold depression in my heart and let anxiety take over my mind. Because I don't deserve to be a part of anyone's life, I'll just end up being a burden.

I'm told cancer is supposed to teach me some life lesson, but I'm sitting here in my grief, and I can't pull myself out. I don't see what I've learned. I can't see beyond today.

Dustin comes over, ignoring my feeble attempt to tell him not to. The guilt of making him my sole confidant eats at my insides. I'm ashamed of putting my pain on him while he stands as sturdy as an oak tree. He sits beside me on the couch and wraps his arms around me. I rest my head on his chest while listening to his rapid heartbeat, the only part of him exposing he's distressed too.

Dustin hasn't had many people to lean on through this experience; he's a casualty of my secrets and isolation. I wish I could help him, give him a lighter, breezy life with bursts of passion and laughter.

I can't offer him much. I'm watered-down and dried up.

today I don't feel like myself
the most unlike myself
unheard, voiceless

I lost me
but it must have been
many days before

for one moment
can't take it all

the slip
/ break
almost went unnoticed

I hope I'm not
forgotten / in the
dead sea

looking for reasons
outside of me

I hope I don't forget
myself
the horizon calls out

SURVIVE/OR/ING

gone under.
cut open.
stitched up.
drink the magic potion
that will make you feel worse
before you feel better.

radioactive status.
airports hate me.
sensors sense me.

I'm still here.
living to tell—
thyroid-less.

crimson blood still crisscrossing
to my heart—
no promises,
always a deadline, a due date.

"cancer survivor"—
doesn't roll off my tongue.
a precarious position
stuck at the back of my throat,
sliding down, cradled in
the unhealed torn tissue
at the base of my neck.

inconceivable.
"survivor," sounds certain,
permanent.

yes, I survived
in this time,
this instance.

I hope I don't slander
what I've been labelled,
allowing the sullen scar
etched across my neck
to fade, to try to forget.

sometimes I stare // at people's necks // checking them // like I can catch it // before it takes over // their life //. like I can save them // I didn't get // to do that for myself

HEART EXPANDING

I'M DRIVING TO THE ADDRESS OF THE THERAPIST I made an appointment with through email. It seemed daunting to comb through the list of accredited therapists in my area, but it was surprisingly easy to choose one.

I was immediately drawn to the therapist's bio photo. Piper Ryan's red frizzy hair framed her delicate pale features, with kind hazel eyes behind tortoiseshell glasses. Her slightly dishevelled hair and minimal makeup balanced out the crispness of her champagne coloured blouse and dark, fitted jeans. She seemed approachable yet serious about her job. Then, when I read her bio, I was sold.

Piper specializes in helping those with health trauma and lives with a long-term health condition herself. I have never considered labelling what I am going through as health trauma but knowing it's her area of expertise makes me feel like she'll understand me.

I pull into a parking spot.

Stomach twisting. Heart retracting.

Fear.

I don't want to do this. I don't want to be here. But I somehow find my hands opening the car door and my feet walking to the building entrance.

As if time snapped forward, I am sitting in her office. It's cozier than I'd expect and quite small. I can hear the ocean from her window—the sound calms me.

Piper makes pleasant small talk at first and then asks me to tell her why I'm here. It's as if I forgot I'd have to share all the thoughts and feelings that are paralyzing.

My eyes burst as I struggle to get the words out.

"I had thyroid cancer...*sob*...and I'm cancer-free now... *gulp*...but I feel like...*sob*...I'm falling apart."

I cry and cry. I haven't cried like this since Dustin picked my avalanche of emotions up off the floor when I found out I had cancer.

Bawling my eyes out in front of a stranger I just met is embarrassing. I'm not even able to articulate why I'm here. It's too hard. I wish I hadn't come.

Piper stares with compassion in her hazel eyes. Her voice is as gentle as the breeze coming through the window.

"Hannah. Put your hands on your lap, and with your fingers, tap your left leg and then your right. Back and forth, just like that. Okay, now take a few deep breaths and close your eyes."

I do as I'm told and feel myself calming down. After Piper leads a few meditation exercises, I'm ready to talk again. We speak about what I went through. How the strength I held for others made it hard to lean on them. The only person I truly let see my vulnerability is Dustin. I'm afraid of cancer coming back. I'm scared of dying.

The session goes by in a flash. I realize I'll need more time in therapy but today is a promising start. Opening up made the pain feel heavier but then, much lighter.

Heart expanding, stomach fluttering.

why did I feel like it was all
up to me? up to me
to make others comfortable
with my disease? make them less
scared of me and what I carried
inside? why did I feel the need
to comfort others
instead of myself?

maybe it was because
I needed to feel like I still
had control. that I had
power over
cancer.

will I
ever let go?

I don't want to forget, but
it's heavy
and it's tainted. like lugging
a sack of bruised apples
up a hill. the apples are no longer
good to eat but I feel obligated
to bring them home
every night. tuck them into
the fridge. preserve them. even though
they'll just get more rotten.

SAVING MYSELF

I'M FINALLY ANGRY. Most of the time, I've been moving between emotional numbness and tidal waves of sadness. But the anger is here now, and I think I enjoy the feeling. I've been poked and prodded. I've been told what to do and how to be. I've been carrying years of my own repressed thoughts and feelings far before cancer showed up. I'm tired of being agreeable and doing what's "right" in the eyes of those who do not know me.

Only I know me.

I'm telling Dustin all of this as we wait at my place for our Indian food order to arrive. He's always been good at dealing with my fiery nature. I think there's a part of him that's happy to see it coming back.

"When people told me, 'Work will be good for you; you need to keep busy,' or 'You look much better; you must be ready to go back to regular life,' I took that seriously. I am tired of fighting with my body and mind to please others."

Dustin looks me straight in the eyes. "You have to do what's right for you. You can't continue to live your life the way others think you should. But, you know, people just say these things sometimes; they don't know the impact. It's really you who is allowing what they say to be your truth." His honesty is hard for my mind to absorb, but his words are more for my soul.

"I don't want it to sound like I'm blaming others. I just—it's hard to go against the grain even if I'm going against myself in the process. I don't know why. I hate it."

My phone rings, I buzz the delivery driver in.

"Well, therapy is such a great start to sorting that out and maybe you can try other things that help you connect back to yourself. You're doing such a great job, My Dear."

"Thank you." I kiss him on the cheek. "I'm so frustrated but I'm ready to work through this. Otherwise, I'm just going to be complaining all the time and that's unattractive," I laugh. I see in his eyes he'll never find me unattractive, unlovable.

I walk to the front door, grab the food, and tip the driver.

Chewing on naan—pistachio chicken curry warming my belly—I look outside my window as crows fly east to roost.

I'm finally in a place where I'm ready to follow a path I set, to stop the cycle that's been suppressing my soul.

Venus retrograde
told me not to cut my hair.

I did it anyway.

I know it's wrong,
but I gorge existential dread—
a temporary satiation.

I don't want to be right.

I attach my hate
to the mirror,
clinging on the morsels
of self-worth.

I question

my own intent.
the words lingering
in the air,
dark and morose.
sucking up the last of the oxygen—
a breathless expiration.

I break off

just to watch it burn.
igniting a fresh wound
that will heal into
a phoenix-shaped scar.

I am for the unknown.

I shed like a molting snake,
the leather no longer my shield.
naked and vulnerable,
expelling all that wronged me.
righting myself,
as I beam
reborn.

these ashen vines are almost dead,
but they climb along the brainwaves,
seeping into my vocal cords.

as I scream,
the green shoots grow,
parting my quivering lips,
they wrap around my tender neck.

these tendrils of buried thought
still live on.

I thought I burnt them.
told them to never come back.
but the seed remained
and waited for a very bad day

to sprout.
to constrict.

now I see them for what they are.
recoil like slapped wrists—

my wrist when I reach
to grab the past and the hate
and the fear.

my wrist when I forget.
my power.

In my subsequent therapy sessions, Piper offers me questions to contemplate. One lingers in my being, surfacing a profound truth.

"Have you ever wondered why you put yourself in the position for others to lean on you?"

I deepen my breath, sitting in that feeling.

"Maybe I like people to lean on me because I'd much rather have others be vulnerable. Vulnerability risks rejection and failure. I fear having anyone see me in that way. I fear losing the value I bring to the people in my life."

There's a glimmer in her eye. Like I've cracked the code.

"Ah, that's it. Value. Without your health, your ability to help other people or be there in a greater capacity was lost. You're now translating that to a false belief that you bring no value to the people in your life and connecting that with your self-image."

My breath catches in my neck.

"Wow. So, that's why I've been isolating myself from people."

"Yes, and here's the thing, Hannah. There's so much inside you to value. Valuing yourself is not about external approval or validation. You find validation from within."

After learning I love to write, she assigns homework to start writing my feelings through poetry.

"Allow poetry to take you on an inner journey. This is where you take your power back."

I seek solace
in the line.

I'm too far fated
for this apothecary.

oracles told me
to carry my bones
with me.

but my body
is sinking through

the cracks.

calling itself home
to the salt and earth.

slipping signets—
a tearing song,
withered and dry.

please forgive me,
body.
I'll speak to you
more sweetly.

SEARCHING

IT'S RAINING, and I'm walking through the cobblestoned streets of Gastown to find where I'll be meeting an astrologer. Now that I realize I'll be in this world for a while longer, and therapy has taken me out of survival mode, I'm very curious about discovering who I am and why I'm on this earth. Maybe learning more about how I'm wired will help bring my power back too.

I find the small alcove to the doorway and make my way up the creaky stairs. I'm nervous because I don't know how to be. I realize I've been avoiding looking at myself as a spiritual person. All I've done during my health journey is try to heal my body, while holding onto this tethered spirit, hoping it doesn't slip away.

The astrologer, Andi, welcomes me in. Then, she asks why I am curious about receiving a reading.

"The moon and the stars have always transfixed me. Watching the light dance in the night sky brings comfort to hard days. Understanding more about myself and how I connect to planetary energies might provide the answers I'm searching for within."

Andi smiles, her blue eyes sparkle. I can tell she's looking forward to reading my chart.

"Wonderful, well, let's get started then!"

She moves her laptop to show her screen—a complicated circular chart of symbols and lines. Andi explains that I'm looking at my natal chart, which shows where the planets were at the exact time I was born. Wide-eyed, I settle in and get ready to learn.

"What I notice first is this T-square with Pluto in Scorpio, right on the ascendant. Super potent. Then connected to Jupiter is your Leo in the ninth house and your Moon in Aquarius in the third."

I watch her outline the T-square as a big triangle expands the edges of my chart.

"With Pluto right there on your ascendant, that speaks to depth. Pluto wants to go deep to understand. It also speaks to courage. If you're open to doing the work, meeting life's difficulties and challenges can be transformative. Doing the work is acknowledging what you've pushed down into the shadows. Pluto is here to help you face what you've avoided or ignored. You can either allow this energy to make you shut down and suffer, or you can allow it to transform you."

I nod as I feel a deep knowing inside urging to push past my fears.

"Part of going into your shadows with Pluto is to bring love, understanding, and compassion—the light—to these parts of you. This contorted uncomfortable energy will then unfurl, and you can use that power in a new way."

I receive her words with another nod. There's a calm awareness in my body that my mind can't comprehend yet.

She moves on to talk about how Pluto, Jupiter, and the Moon are connected in my chart.

"The opposition between your Moon and Jupiter really speaks to writing, communication, the mind, thinking, spirituality, learning, and teaching. Jupiter in the ninth house is also all about travel! I see you also have the Sun, Mercury, and Venus in Sagittarius, so travel is where you feel more like yourself."

"Yes!" Here's one fact I know for sure.

"This T-Square is showing that you are on a soul journey. An eternal quest to always expand and grow by following your inner guidance."

As Andi explains more about these lines and symbols in my chart, I'm beginning to see the beauty of the journey I'm on. The trauma and afflicting emotions are all part of expanding in some way.

An hour and a half go by quickly. I leave feeling connected to myself and wanting more.

born.
imum coeli—
bottom of the sky.

I'm here,
but hidden.

the top of the sky
is heavenly, ethereal.
the bottom is where
souls meet to decide
their fate.

where kept secrets
wait to be tapped—
shooting up
free from
the shadows.

souls shine
when they've spent
time at the bottom.

I'm spending time
trudging with the shadows
through into the light.

EMOTIONAL AUDIT

I KNOW I'VE ISOLATED MYSELF—being reclusive is my coping mechanism. Although choosing solitude has made me independent and resilient in many ways, I also see how it's backfired, hurting my spirit. Therapy and spiritual practices are allowing me to go within and see more clearly.

I've been keeping my voice hidden all these years, controlling how I'm perceived—seeking validation and approval to gauge my worth. I'm sick of it all. It made me sick too.

In the next step of my inner journey, I decide I should try reiki. I've only recently heard about reiki energy healing and have no clue what that means, but I'm curious to find out. I google reiki practitioners in my area and find one who also does Angel Life Coaching (Mediumship). I'm intrigued. I book a session.

Lying on a massage table inside a small apartment room, I feel slightly ill being reminded about all the examination tables I've laid on this year. But here, I feel safe. There's a glass of water with strawberries in it and chocolate truffles in a bowl to enjoy when the session ends. A pleasant scent of freshly cut grass wafts through the open window, and nature sounds with soft chimes play on the speakers in the corner of the room.

Melanie, the Reiki Master and certified Archangel Life Coach and Angelic Medium walks into the room smiling, brown curls bouncing at her shoulders.

"Are you ready to begin?"

"Yes." I angle my neck up to look her in the eyes, not knowing what I'm saying yes to but trusting I'm here for a reason.

Melanie's hands hover over my body, moving around at my head and slowly making their way down to my feet. In certain areas, she stops, eyes fixed, she lets out yips and yelps. I don't know what to think and try to stay out of my mind—in case uncomfortable laughter comes out. Biting my cheek, I re-centre. She continues, and I sweat through my jeans and knit tank top. I feel energy radiating out of me.

The session ends, and I'm light-headed—now I understand why water and chocolate are necessary after the session. Melanie goes over what she found.

"There is a blockage at your feet; you've been living in your head too much."

I agree.

"Your ears have a large buffer around them, but there's some debris from negative self-talk and potentially internalizing criticism."

Eyes wide. "That makes sense."

"You are overwhelmed from expressing and repressing emotion. You put on a strong face, but these repressed emotions need to be seen and acknowledged. Are you hiding from friends and family, trying to be stoic?"

I lower my gaze and tell her how I had thyroid cancer. How I didn't share my emotions because I thought that's how I could protect people. But really, I'm learning I was scared to reveal my true self in fear of being rejected. I'm trying to be more open now.

"You're storing these emotions and memories in your energy body. You need to release this to feel more like yourself, but at the same time, feel like someone completely new. You're going through a time where you don't quite know who you are anymore. Currently, you're on a spirit-ual path to learn from this period of illness on a soul level."

I feel Melanie's words flutter in my heart space as they click truths into my being.

She goes on to say how I need to practice sending love and healing to my neck, throat, and vocal cords—thanking this area of my body for all it's done instead of casting it aside.

I tell her it won't be easy, but I'll try.

The last piece of wisdom she shares is that she wants me to journal my sadness—an emotional audit. Breaking down the events, people, and situations that made me sad throughout this lifetime will help acknowledge the pain I've held in my body—the reasons I've felt so disconnected from my mind, body, and soul.

And so, I do. I go home and write about how I built protection around my pure and gentle soul from a young age. Always wanting to do the "right" thing, I didn't feel like I was free to express myself. I learned to behave, speak when I was told, hide my emotions if they were ugly—no one wants to love or deal with an outspoken, wild girl.

young girl whispers
26 screams
echoes since 8

listen to
Me

inner truth
in broken chords

plaster and paint
check vital
force

My fingers clench my pen, aching, but I continue to write about how I had a hard time relating to other kids. I never felt like I could act like myself and be accepted because when I did, I would be made fun of or not included. I was also scared of getting into trouble, always looking for validation from adults.

After learning astrology, I now know my Aquarius moon, which rules my emotions, is partly to blame. Aquarians can feel eccentric and like outsiders but also desperately want to be included. That's me to a tee.

To ensure I had friends, I'd overcompensate, catering to their needs and not always asking for the same in return, and fearing rejection carried into adulthood whether it had to do with school, work, relationships, family dynamics, or my social life. I listened to my parents, to people older than me, and took their opinions as facts instead of contemplating what was true in my own human experience. As I developed a perfectionist attitude, no one could see the cracks under my façade. I started not to notice the cracks either.

After an hour of writing, I'm not done with my emotional audit, but the cramps in my hands tell me that's enough for one day. There are pieces of me I've left unattended and ignored so I didn't have to remember the emotional pain. It's my duty to myself to continue the work now.

I translated the superficial
for palpability. smothered.
my voice. in exchange
for acceptance.

now plain to see.

young adult years. caught.
an inimical ritual.
deafening to
my intuition, it took

cancer to wake up.

old me struggled to
accept herself. to love herself.
had no choice but to

face herself. reveal the parts
she hid for surface validation,
external expectation.

she hid in her shell
from opinions
and rejection. burdened
with the need for approval.

now

I shake the shell when
I show up for others
and not for myself.

the worst thing is being
uncomfortable with yourself
to allow others to feel
comfortable with you.

CRACK OPEN

sometimes when I yawn
my neck muscles
gets stuck
for a second
I think
they'll never go back
again
I touch my neck and remember
how much I've been through
how delicate I still am

I was stubborn in the wrong way. I was holding on to a perceived strength, like a shell unable to crack. If I give it a chance, a faint peek of light and air, maybe I'll learn to be stubborn in a new way.

Here I am now—unlearning. I'm unlearning the human I became. The person who assumed showing up in the world how I thought others wanted to see me was more important than showing up for me. I now give people a chance to embrace me for who I am.

Here I am now—learning. I'm learning to listen to my inner voice. I'm learning to be so genuinely me that nothing can take me away from living my truth.

I am holding on to the vulnerability of being human. Allowing what I need and desire to seep into my soul.

VISIONS

GROWING UP, MY MOM WOULD READ MY TEA LEAVES. She learned it from her mom—my grandma—and now I'm starting to learn from her. As a child, I never thought of tea leaves as a spiritual activity. I used to just think of it as entertainment. But, the tea leaves never lie.

As summer's embers paint the trees crimson, I'm outside by the warmth of my parents' firepit. My mom sets up a s'mores station and brings over a hot cup of loose-leaf orange pekoe tea. Sipping the tea, I think of my life and how I'm proud of the changes happening inside me. I want something else but can't put my finger on it. I hope the tea leaves can give a glimpse into what direction I should go.

My intentions swirl with the tea leaves. I finish my last sip, filtering the liquid through my teeth to not get grainy leaves in my mouth. Then I close my eyes, put the teal teacup with miniature gold-flaked flowers face down on the saucer, and turn it three times towards my heart.

Handing the cup and saucer over to my mom without looking inside my cup, I feel wishful. The warmth of the tea still heating my core, giving me something to believe in.

"OH!" My mom exclaims.

She always says that the first time she looks in my cup. I'm used to her endearing dramatics. Bracing myself for the messages to come, I sit still, watching her work her magic.

"I see a book next to a plane at the bottom of your cup. Maybe you're making plans to travel somewhere in the next six months?"

I have been researching New Zealand.

"I also see a crescent moon near the top of your cup. Right

now, you're very receptive to change and spend a lot of time in introspection."

I nod.

"There's also a paddle boat next to a galloping horse. I think this means after a difficult journey, you'll eventually know what you're aiming for."

"That would be nice," I laugh.

She mentions a few more visions—an elephant that signifies the wisdom I'm gaining, a turtle for taking things slowly. And a large smiling bullfrog that shows the pride and romance in my relationship with Dustin.

Sometimes I think the images she foretells are because she's my mom, not because she's reading the leaves. But I like to believe what she says anyway.

A few weeks later, my mom, who's coming with me to pick out crystals and having long discussions about my new revelations, surprises me by booking a crystal sound bowl meditation. Mom knows I've been curious about sound baths and the meditative qualities these quartz crystal bowls bring.

When we arrive at the studio, two zero-gravity fold-out chairs and eye pillows await us next to seven different-sized crystal bowls. The sound practitioner welcomes us; her eyes sparkle with excitement. Settling into the chairs and placing the satin pillows over our eyes, she begins with a few breathing exercises. Then the sounds start.

I see the colours of the crystal tones in my mind's eye. Bright blue, then indigo, flashes in a never-ending space, expanding and collapsing like a black hole. Then comes pink, orange, and yellow. I'm watching an extraordinary dance of light with no physical light in front of me.

Not only do I see colours, but I also feel the sound vibrations from the different bowls she's playing. My body relaxes, my mind calms, immersed in my senses. The deeper the notes get, the slower my brainwaves move. The higher the sounds get, the more in tune I feel with something larger than myself. The sensation is euphoric.

After the session, I feel present with myself—connected. Calming your mind can heal your body; calming your body can heal your mind.

RECALIBRATING

IN THE DIMLY LIT MEDITATION CENTRE, I find a padded seat on the floor near the back. My notebook and pen are ready on my lap as instructed by Bree, the spiritual medium leading the intuition class. A slow trickle of people streams in. I gaze out the large arched window framed by hanging copper gongs, rain falling on the North Shore mountains.

Bree walks in, brown wavy bob grazing her shoulders. Bliss beams from her eyes to her smile, and radiates as she flows into the room. She's wearing culottes, a white t-shirt, and simple gold rings with a delicate gold chain around her neck—she doesn't look like the eccentric spiritual mediums you see in the movies. She says hello and tells us how much she loves coming to Vancouver. Then, Bree begins to tell us about herself.

"As a child, I was psychic. Through the practical nature of this world, I shut off my intuitive senses until my curiosities around meditation, quantum healing, and self-help slowly opened me back up to realigning with my soul."

She shares what that journey looked like, bringing in the tangible understanding for folks like me who have no clue how soul alignment feels. At first, she studied business, joking that she liked pencil skirts and travel. Then, she followed her dreams of training in dance in Los Angeles. From there, she found a spiritual community that felt accessible to her, learning how to meditate and eventually reconnecting with her psychic abilities. Since then, intuition has been a driving force in everything she does.

"By allowing big jumps of trust and faith, I'm living the full expression of myself. I'm here today to support you in finding the power of your intuition—a clear connection with your soul."

Bree takes us through a series of meditation practices. In one, I get paired up with a woman named Simone. She has long brown hair that goes all the way down to her waist and piercing green eyes. She's wearing yoga pants and a flowy shirt, just like me. Locking my blue eyes with her greens, we smile and sense a mutual trust as we are about to embark on an energy exchange.

"Have you ever been to Bree's class before?" I ask.

"No, I haven't. I'm actually an intuitive healer, so I like to go to classes like these to strengthen my skills."

She asks why I decided to go to the class.

"I feel like I have good intuition but tend to ignore it. I'm hoping to find tools to sort through what's true within myself so I can start to feel more confident using my intuition."

"I think you will!" She smiles.

Bree's soft voice breaks through our chatter. She tells us to sit face-to-face with our partners and close our eyes. Sitting cross-legged with my spine straight, trying to mimic Simone's poise, the smell of incense snaking through the air, I feel uneasy and out of place. *Should I even be here? Is this too out there for me?*

Breathing deeply, I push through my thoughts and refocus. Bree begins by leading us through different prompts, allowing us to journey into each others' energies.

At first, I feel antsy. Then all of a sudden, my body calms and I see Simone in my mind. She's in a meditative state, floating in a desert with palm trees, succulents, and white light surrounding her. I wonder if I'm making it up in my head when Bree tells us to open our eyes and share what we experienced.

After Simone hears what I saw, her green eyes widen as she says, "That is exactly what I envision when I do my meditations."

I'm in awe.

A part of me is recalibrating, shifting my perspective from old me to something new. All I've believed, or better yet, restricted myself to believe, is based on a reality that society created and stories I made for myself out of fear.

mind reaches
up to soul
come home

let's unite
live in this space
this thin thread
can be replaced

by a stronger tether
we're more powerful
together

A month later, I'm sitting in an astrology circle led by Andi, surrounded by like-minded people. We're laughing and connecting. We're sharing some of the deepest parts of ourselves as we read each other's charts. I never thought I'd be here, enjoying something so intimate with people I barely know. But here I am, attending an astrology class, feeling safe and secure in my own knowing. I'm following the lead of those who are willing to bare their souls.

I am coming home to myself.

Astrology and intuition practices are helping me learn how to navigate the path back to myself. It's the inner knowing. The reconnecting. The exploring. The journey no one else can take but me. What could be a more exciting adventure than learning to understand myself better?

LOST AND FOUND

and I'm ever-changing
but I'm not erasing
the things I've done
because they've shown me
what I've overcome

Life stretches on and I've been in therapy for two months. At times I feel like I've lost my sense of self and in other moments I feel so much conviction for the woman I am—for the woman I'm becoming.

I've lost the identity I once clung to and that's a good thing. Instead of trying to control the future, I'm adapting to focusing on the here and now.

Every second, I can choose how I want to feel. Every second, my feelings change. Or even fuse together. I will laugh then tack on some sadness, some anxiety. I grieve and then comes a smile, eyes squinting, grateful. Constantly, I am changing. I'm welcoming the feelings while also turning them away.

How can life be complicated, yet simple? I'm lost while finding myself.

what a beautiful weird day
in this magical twisted life
I welcome what comes
always turn my face
up to the sun
and the rain
it's ok to feel it
all
in the same day

this healing
oh the
h e a l i n g
is a lovely
nonsensical
agonizing
unfurling
predicament
that's brought
unexplainable answers
only my soul
can comprehend

I'm having brunch with my friend Korry. She's been very supportive during this time when I feel vulnerable, opening my heart and soul—learning to love my body again, too.

She listens as I talk about what I've been learning about myself and what I no longer want in my life.

"It's now easy to see how I've been conditioned toward inauthenticity. I can see it in others also. I've lost friends because we have nothing in common now. I also lost myself at times. These losses first felt debilitating, but now it's kind of freeing. I have the impulse to start from scratch and burn everything else down." I laugh.

Korry's eyes widen with a mixed expression of surprise and understanding.

A mischievous smile spreads across my face. "Don't worry, I won't."

She laughs but then looks at me intently.

"Don't forget to be kind to yourself. You've already been through so much change."

"There are times I get impatient. But I can't just quit everything I don't like and run away from it all. I have to take the time to sort through what I want out of my life."

"And there's no rush." She smiles, sipping her coffee.

EGO < CONSCIOUSNESS

THE THYROID MEDICATION HAS BEEN COURSING through my body for a year now. I have more energy, and I love how I can be active and not feel like I need to nap after. At work, I'm learning my job title and external praise do not define me. I'm stricter about when I start and finish work for the day, realizing all these expectations were self-imposed, thinking people were always watching, judging me.

I also have a whole new priority now—my inner self. During the winter, I practiced meditation, read poetry and self-help books, joined an astrology club, took a tarot card reading course, and travelled to New Zealand. These new experiences are helping me find a way out of anxious intellect and into calm consciousness—allowing me to crack open a little more, letting the light in.

I invite my friend Sinead to a breathwork class. It's taken a while to open up and expose my spiritual, vulnerable parts to my family and friends. But, each time I bring a loved one into my new world, I get to see how I'm received. Despite some who don't understand, I'm beginning to see my revealing allows a stronger connection with the ones growing in their own ways too.

Sinead and I walk to the address written on our tickets. Earlier, when we read about the class, we weren't sure what to think as it came with the caveat—it's a transcendental experience. As we turn the corner, I squint through the sunlight to see an old three-storey warehouse with peeling paint and dirty windows. I feel as though we might be lost, but we continue to the door where a greeter awaits us.

Although it's a warm spring day, he fits a typical East Vancouver uniform in his all-black outfit—jeans, leather jacket, and Vans canvas sneakers.

He checks our tickets and directs us up the three flights of stairs. As we walk up, I smell a hint of mold and wonder if I'll be inhaling unwelcome particles during a class that's all about breathing.

At the opening of the staircase, I catch a glimpse of the space we'll be inhabiting for the next hour and a half. Wooden beams, soft light shining through gauzy curtains moving with the breeze coming through the open windows, potted greenery, and hanging plants—it's serene. It also smells fresh up on the third floor, diffusers expelling fragrance reminiscent of mountain air.

Our instructor, Bree, awaits us with smiling eyes. Sinead checks in first, and I follow. I want to mention to Bree that I've been to her intuition class before, but I'm feeling shy and just say hello. She echoes hello back with song in her voice but looks at me with intensity. I feel like she recognizes me, or maybe she knows something about me I don't.

After taking off our shoes and grabbing our pens and notebooks—as instructed in the pre-class email—we amble into a larger room. It's just as airy and welcoming but also quite overwhelming as my eyes take in close to one hundred black padded gym mats spaced out on the floor. We find a spot that's not too close to the front but not so far away that we won't see Bree.

Sinead and I chat away as more people trickle in.

I say to Sinead, "Are you nervous? I feel nervous."

"Yeah, I've never been to something like this!"

I raise my eyebrows and purse my lips.

"I hope I haven't taken you to something too wild," I grin.

We both laugh, clutching our notebooks, as Bree begins to greet us all. We hear about her journey, just as she mentioned in her intuition class, and I begin to relax. I need to trust this.

Then comes the warning.

"Breathwork is transcendental. We use our active breath to calm the body and mind. This may be painful for some of you—both physically and emotionally. But, by the end, you will be in a place of healing, closer to your intuition, and some of us may find a link between our physical body and the spiritual world. There are three of us here today to check on you—to remind you to continue, to push past the discomfort."

Breathwork sounds overwhelming. I peer over at Sinead but see in her demeanour that she's ready to try it out, and I realize it's too late to back out now.

Bree starts to show us the patterned breath and asks us to follow.

"Breathe in the stomach, in the chest, out through the mouth—we'll repeat this for forty-five minutes."

We then lie down on our mats to copy the breathing repetition she's set out for us. At first, I find it easy. It also sounds incredible as I hear my own breath and almost a hundred others echoing the same sounds around the room—like a wind machine. Then comes the wailing. Above my breath, I hear others crying out in pain. I don't understand until a few minutes later, my hands, which are resting at my sides, begin to cramp. Not painful enough to cry out but enough to understand how others may be feeling.

I can't tell how much time has passed; it could be five minutes or forty. I kind of want this to end. As I think that, Bree tells us we're halfway through. She asks us to take one moment to let out our pain and all scream up into the ether, then return to our breath.

As more minutes tick by, I start to feel my face twitch, muscles spasming. I hear Sinead next to me and I can tell she's in pain. At that moment, a woman helping with the class comes by to check on us. Placing her hands on my shoulders and collar bone, telling me I can do this. I feel comfort knowing we're in a safe space. And, we're all in this together as my eardrums move from my internalized breath to the unified breath swirling around.

Just as I think I can't go any longer, Bree tells us to slow our breath. She leads us through meditation. I feel my body calm—ethereal and airy. There's a light within me. It's journeyed from the cosmos and connected my body with the core of the earth. I'm everything and nothing. All-seeing, all-knowing. Simply existing as the Universe moves through me.

We are asked to roll up to a seated position, take out our notebook and pen. Bree prompts us to write a letter to our souls. The words flow.

Dearest Soul,

I'm ready to release the person I am no longer supposed to be. I'm ready to let go of the expectations I put on myself due to conditioning. I will listen to You. I'm ready to understand what lights me up. I feel scared, but I'd rather take a leap of faith with the Universe than do nothing at all. I need help honouring that. I need help to see the way. I am ready to embody my true purpose and take the journey towards what I really need. I'm willing to receive wisdom from the Universe and be fully present and content in my everyday life. I'm finally ready to step into my authentic self, into a place where I respect every part of the life I lead.

Before my pen leaves the paper, she asks us to write how our soul would respond. I take one deep breath and continue.

- *Be in your body more*
- *Make morning meditation a priority to connect to your intuition*
- *Find space for yourself*
- *Write a book*

Heart flutters.

- *You've prepared yourself for this time, so you can create*

Eyes widening.

- *You have so much to be grateful for, and you have the privilege to live the life you want to create if you give yourself a chance*

As if these words were channelled from something bigger than my mind, I stare at the pen scratch. Emotions rush to my head. All these months of searching for understanding inside have boiled down to a few bullet point answers from my soul after one breathwork class.

Maybe too much oxygen has gone to my brain, but there's universal love and deep knowing that fills my heart space, replenishing the frenetic emptiness that used to stifle my breath.

I didn't know if I was ready

I walked along the stars
looking for answers
chased the moon
breathed rhythms
sought meaning in symbols
adorned myself in crystals
read books filled with lessons
and recalled memories
of struggles overcome

I sat in silence
questioning myself
until one day
I knew it didn't matter
if I was ready
I deserved the life I wanted

I deserve the life I'm not ready for

MIRRORS

I GO OUT FOR DINNER with my friends Kaylee, Leanne, and Heather. I feel emboldened seeing myself in a new way. I share the journey I've been on—talking about therapy, astrology, reiki, and breathwork.

It feels good to no longer search the faces of others to see if I'm accepted. I accept the vulnerable words that flow through and validate them as my power.

But, with these three, I don't need to worry about my choice of words anyway. They are genuinely happy for me. I feel unconditional support for the person I am—imperfection and all. My sharing invites them to open up, confiding in the struggles and learning they've experienced, too.

With love in our eyes, we clink our wine glasses to personal growth and leave the night in a tight group hug. I'm feeling closer to my friends because I'm less fearful of sharing my truth, my soul.

I chiselled once
impenetrable stone
to reveal
a mirror

reflections dance
I speak words so
vulnerable
others see themselves

in me
come closer
face-to-face

we lean in
to this knowing
together
holding hands
with surrender

CROWS USED TO VISIT ME

THE CROWS HAVE LEFT ME ALONE for quite some time. Occasionally I look out my window, remembering their foreboding presence while noticing their absence, the same way I swallow and no longer feel that familiar pressure on my neck. Today, as I look out my window, I watch three ladybugs crawl down the pane. The week before, Dustin and I found two ladybugs in the living room, flying around and crawling on the ceiling.

I search the spiritual meaning of ladybugs and find they symbolize renewal and transformation. I tell Dustin later in the evening, and he smiles, giving me a big kiss. It's nice to know he'll always embrace my ever-changing existence with my new perspectives and beliefs.

Life is starting to feel easier and lighter—ladybug light. Something has changed inside me, and it's not just because I no longer have a thyroid. I feel different. I'm more connected to the Universe than I ever was because I'm more connected to myself. I spend time listening to the messages that come to me as I close my eyes and feel a bright light reach the crown of my head and stream through my feet.

Crows used to visit me, now ladybugs do.

voice box
locked in neck
crawling, gripping

conditioning
drowns the innate

be a good girl

value approval
till blue in the face

slice along
knife's neck edge
between body
and mind

dark ominous clouds
vent vice
crows circle
the canyon

clear the opening
come up for air

be the force
you are

ladybugs climb
fluttering along
seraphic notes

key's right here
always been here

unlock from
within

soul song
threads
the horizon

SIFT ME

CANCER MADE ME FEEL LIKE EVERYTHING was falling apart. I was grabbing onto fragments of my existence as they floated into the ether. It wasn't until time moved on and I grasped what happened that I realized cancer didn't arrive in my life to make me lose myself and everything that makes me, me.

Cancer came along and sifted the sands of my life. It took away what no longer served me—releasing me from the sandbox and rolling me onto the beach and into the vast ocean. But it also reformed some sands and made them into exquisite rocks and crystals, revealing the sacred support from loved ones and the magical depths of my being.

It showed me that the most beautiful, brilliant, soul-affirming life cannot be held or contained. Not by me, not by anyone.

I had to let go of the ending—
the perfectly packaged pieces of life
collection of control inside

I had to let go

once the words "I have cancer"
were released from my lips
I had to let go

so I could be free

so my life could change and
go up—and down—and through

allow myself the dignity
to walk through this life
ever-changing

from
experience

to
knowing

I don't stand
I h o v e r

I lay in the space of
the burning and breaking
to reignite this soul
once held in shackles

cancer freed me
I had to let
go to see the beginning

she stamps down
on the dirt

the foundations
of her soul
settle with the soil

grounded and sure
she roots
arms sway
embracing the air

hair lifts in the wind
she's all freedom and fire
blazing without a care

she's held by the earth
her core is fire too
and it feeds her soul
and checks her mind

before
her embers ignite

FREE AS A BIRD

IT'S BEEN THREE YEARS SINCE I HAD CANCER. I've lived the last three years learning to remember the pain I went through so I can healthily cope. And, most importantly, recognizing the pain I created when I wasn't true to myself.

Although I've changed a lot, there are a few things that will always stay the same—my love for Dustin and my love for travel. Two years ago, Dustin and I moved in together and added two fur babies, Earl Grey and Lady Willow—our adorable British Shorthair cats. I always enjoyed living alone—I had for many years prior, but cancer made me realize how ready I was to share more of my life with Dustin. He was ready too. Life is too short to wait for the ideal moment or follow the perfect steps. We had to follow our hearts.

I also achieved my goal of setting foot on each of the seven continents. Although, I still need to travel around Australia, as I only spent a brief moment there.

Having already been to countries in North America, Europe, and Asia, I planned trips to countries nearby the remaining four continents. I frolicked on Fiordland in New Zealand, drank organic wine in Chile, waddled beside penguins in Antarctica, and sipped refreshing mint tea in Morocco.

Being with friends in New Zealand and experiencing Chile and Antarctica with my mom was really special. But, in true fashion, for the last continent—Africa—I went on my own. Arriving in Morocco shortly after quitting my job, completely unaware of what was ahead, other than having plans to write a book, felt exhilarating.

Travel after cancer taught me one of the most important lessons of all. That embracing the unknown frees you.

I crave freedom so I tell myself every day:
I am free.

I am free. I am free. I am free.

What a gift to exist beyond the boundaries—
cutting constrictions. Because the words
escape my lips into the air.

I am free.

PADDED YEARS

I DRIVE THROUGH THE STREET, scanning for parking. I'm right by the medical imaging centre where I had my first ultrasound. The reminder of that experience haunts my neck. There seems to be construction everywhere I turn. I had planned to be on time, early even. But time has other plans for me.

After searching for what feels like forever but is more like four minutes, I find a spot to park and jump out, racing to my appointment. Running up the steps, I realize I'm in the wrong section of the building. Panting, I run back down, find the proper entrance and barrel through the automatic sliding doors—the receptionist stares, uninterested in my parking problems.

It's my three-year check-up. For three years, I have lived taking a pill every morning that tricks my body into thinking I still have a thyroid. I take a combination of seven more vitamins and medications throughout the day so my limbs and lips don't tingle and go numb. Every six months, I get a blood test to check my levels; every six months, I hold my breath.

My endocrinologist, Doctor Sunda, is waiting. He does not seem to be bothered that I'm late and welcomes me with a smile. I like him. He always takes his time to answer the questions I ask. I'm glad I found him because there's no way I was staying with Doctor Wagner, who was very much qualified but did my thyroid biopsy as if I were a specimen. Old me would have felt like I had to remain loyal to a medical professional; now I do what's right for me.

Eyes steady behind his rectangular doctor-looking glasses, he says, "Hannah, your blood test came back clear. I'm thrilled your TSH level is low."

After three years, I know TSH stands for thyroid stimulating hormone, and the medication dose I take must be large enough to suppress it.

"Oh, good!"

I'm relieved, but the relief is padded, as if I just fell onto a giant bean bag chair—knowing it's still important I get to the five-year mark. That's when the chance of cancer coming back is lowered.

"How are you feeling?"

"I've been doing pretty well. This year I'm less tired and my limbs don't go tingly as often. Although, I feel like my memory isn't as good. I also have irregular periods every month."

"Some of these issues are because we do have to give you a higher dose. We need to remain aggressive with the medication for two more years. But, please keep me in the loop if you are concerned or have symptoms worsen."

I nod, thanking him.

Leaving Doctor Sunda's office, I call Dustin right away.

"Hey, Dude!" I say affectionately.

"Hello, My Dear."

"So, yep, I'm all healthy. Three-year check-up went well!" Knowing I'll never be perfectly healthy, but it's easier to say it that way.

"That's wonderful. Great news! We'll have to celebrate tonight."

We leave the call saying, "I love you."

Then I call my mom. She wants to celebrate too.

I never want to let myself feel too happy or too sad about my health, knowing there are unknowns every step of the way. But, through all I've learned about myself these past few years, I know that despite the worries I may hold for the rest of my life, I'll always have faith that the Universe has set out the path I'm meant to take.

Celebrating each year being cancer-free feels foreign. But, I acknowledge and honour the experience for helping me see myself more clearly. I will always celebrate me.

dear Universe,
I find myself looking at the stars a lot. I chase
the moon most nights and soak in
the horizon each morning. do you
feel my energy? will you
share yours with me?
I trust you, Universe. take me

LIFE CYCLE

Love the flowers blooming up my spine
embrace the dark new moon in my third eye
inhale the ocean breeze as I stretch
where I rest
exhale in forested trees

It's easy to lapse into old patterns of fear—forgetting that power and tenderness are one and the same. I am as delicate and strong as the earth. My eyes shoot open right before night turns to day. At first oblivious calm, then habitual fear, then conscious surrender. A cycle I'll flow through maybe forever. In these moments, I remind myself to let go, to come home to myself. I no longer carry the fear so close. It's merely an observation.

I sat outside all morning
a slow simmer
the sun changed my prickled
cool skin to a glistening dew
I took the morning in
with a soulful silence

observing the Universe
as it moved around me
and I moved through it

this morning is all I need
and it's nothing
but a surrender
to here and now

My world is deliciously different. Because I tormented myself for so long, I lived in fear for too long. My body showed me reality checks are necessary so I can pause to remember who I am.

What hurt me, how I hurt myself, has shown me the beauty in simplicity and the value of gratitude. It leads to more than I'd ever know if I had never had cancer and life didn't challenge me.

I believe that those who go through a traumatic experience and are willing to face their egos and open their minds have the opportunity to connect with the intangible magic of the heavens. The balanced duality of both darkness and light.

When you go through an experience like mine, you *feel* through the world rather than move through the world, for some time. This period can provide access to an intangible magic of understanding more than the physical world.

There are realms of light and magic and messages only for the ears of those who've been through something terrible and terrifying—a consolation of constellations sharing pieces of the Universe with you, as you shared more than enough with it.

UNIVERSE EXTENSION

I go back
to the forest
by the sea

to remind myself
what it means

to be held so gently
and loved so dearly

by my soul on this earth

to feel alive
eternally
and unconditionally

I love myself more fully now. I harness an undying love for who I am because I learned that love nurtures my pure voice within.

I had to go through trauma that no one I knew had experienced before, so I couldn't turn to anyone but myself—breaking free of listening to others to know what was right for me.

I've listened to each layer of myself—Mind, Body, Soul—taken note of their grievances and weaved them into an infinite braid that exists within intuition, vulnerability, and self-love.

I love myself because I realize I will not lose my soul when the time comes to leave this body. I will be a deep extension of the Universe. And the Universe is never-ending.

the stars
reflect in her eyes

lives she's lived before
stare down at her
burning bright pathways

all the answers are within

there is a piece of her
in the constellations in the sky
in the air she breathes
a piece planted in the earth
swimming in the sea
a piece in the smoke as the
fire cracks her soul to life
the atoms inside her
are the same atoms
that make the Universe

she is one and the same
apart and together

WHO WILL I BE AFTER IT ALL?

MAYBE I'LL FALL BACK INTO OLD HABITS, forgetting what's changed inside. Maybe I'll climb into new territory, uprooting everything I thought I'd be. Or maybe, I'll be a little bit of both until what I redefine and what I keep is who I'm meant to be. Transformation holds hands with surrender, after all.

ego strapped
in the back
seat

eager to take
the wheel
full throttle

tread carefully
biorhythm
can reverse

check blindspots
there with bells

on the radio
appears in the static

turn the volume down
separate
from the noise

leave space to
manoeuvre
variables ahead

This period in my life has taught me that it's essential to know the difference between following paths meant for others versus listening to their wisdom. I plan to follow my intuition in everything I do, but I'll always appreciate the advice and opinions from loved ones and others my inner voice guides me to trust.

I'm thankful I have a community around me that celebrates personal growth. Holding onto ego will not allow evolution. It will only stifle the bright light within me, bleed inauthenticity into my relationships, and take away my power.

Letting go is hard. Sometimes it's more painful than the actual torment of holding onto my trauma. But, through faith in myself, I walked—at times, crawled—through the grief and eventually found my way. My inner voice led me to therapy and spiritual teachings, a path my mind couldn't quite connect to at first, but my body and soul intuitively required.

Now letting go is a ritual. It doesn't happen overnight. It's a slow peeling of layers, of realizations, of acceptance. It's about each intentional breath I take. The way I wake up in the morning with gratitude and surrender and a forever trust that I'm on the right path.

I'll shed the external noise around me every day if it means I can be closer to hearing my soul. I'll write love letters to my soul every day if it means I can unravel my truth.

All these moments of life that I used to hold onto are much more beautiful when I allow them to pass through me. So, who will I be after it all? I'm excited to find out.

stretched twine
amidst
fear—joy
sickness—health

sun rise—set
spun glass
compass
hemisphere
east—west blurs

it's all connected

but time extends
evermore

wellness hums
intersects
soul—body—mind
love is here
to stay

Two and a half years ago, my therapist, Piper, sent me an email quoting something I said after a session. I revisit it often as a reminder:

"I think I'm coming into my true Self. And that takes time. I'm learning to be kind when I get frustrated with myself. My natural intuition is something I am becoming more confident with. I'm learning that I'm allowed to change my perspective and approach to different situations because I'm learning to trust myself. I don't have to stick to the person I thought I was. I can grow and expand."

I always knew my truth; I was always on the right path. But back then, I only had hints of an inner voice. Now it's an embodied knowing.

One day it clicks. I see now that the journey into my breakdown held the same energy as my awakening. But instead of ignoring my inner voice, I listened. It's how the days compounded into months. And just like the day I felt I had slipped away, one morning I woke up and realized I had crossed over from the shadows into pure light. There was no definite time or answer to show me how I passed the threshold. Only signs of crows and ladybugs, of citrine light on the horizon, and the gentle whispers of all the life I've lived, the lessons I've carried, and the pain, too—no longer a sad reminder but a sign of my power.

It's clear now that cancer was the alarm bell to look inward. It gave me a second chance to see life through a new lens—to see my Self. The answers were always deep within; cancer helped me find the tools for the messages to reach the surface.

this ocean breath
won't drown.
tattered messages
escaping these lips
in a current so strong,
it could change rock
to sand.

pebbles under my feet.
I stand with the mountains.
healing light pouring
like raindrops.

as the sun shines
above my head,
and a rainbow joins
my third eye,

oh honey,
I'm powerful.
oh honey,
it's because I'm free:

CITRINE HORIZON

I OPEN MY EYES AND STRETCH. It's a new day. I take my thyroid pill with a big glass of water, press my feet into the soft carpet, and sit in quiet gratitude.

It's dark, but I know the light will be coming through the windows soon. Dustin's slightly smiling in his sleep; I tip-toe around the bed to give him a kiss on the cheek before getting dressed. Petting Earl and Willow as they trace figure eights around my legs, I feed them breakfast and then walk down to the pier, watching for that line of light.

In stillness, I breathe. In and out, in and out. As the ocean shimmers, the first light of the sun pierces the morning. Mesmerizing.

I touch my scar. No need to cover it any more. Feeling its grooves, I lay my hand there and close my eyes as I inhale salt air and soft light.

faint light of dawn
soars over horizon

find scar
dewy and bright

watch citrine light
drawing reminder with eyes

along neck

reaching sea and sky

an apparition stitched up
fading with sunrise

line tucks into ethereal glow
when sun dips behind ocean

honouring Mind Body Soul
opening to Universe

the horizon
is the beginning
and the end
the hope
the clear path
the end of sight
to the eternal light
the horizon brings me home
transports me to the unknown
it's the piece of longing
in my heart
the line
sketched upon my neck
it's my reflection
in his eyes
the horizon slices through

despair and ecstasy .
where the seafoam kisses the sky
the horizon is your arms
outstretched reaching to hold another
the horizon all around us
part of us
chanting
there's always a beyond
there's always
a new light
a new day
a new choice
a new way

AFTERWORD

I WOVE THESE PIECES AND POEMS TOGETHER in 2020, a year that began with a whole new way of seeing the world. I pulled myself into a painful past while living in an uncomfortable present. Both past and present reveal the necessary struggle for a better mindset and better actions, for seeing my truth and personal responsibility in my choices and privilege.

I've learned to embrace situations out of my control. I do not fight the current. I learn from each experience and act in accordance. I try to receive the lessons even when I'm in deep emotional or physical pain. Through the lessons, the wounded places are slowly filled with the love I have for myself, the gratitude I practice, and the wisdom I gain.

Thank you for reading my story. I hope it touches you and that you're reminded to always listen to the layers of yourself: Mind, Body, and Soul; to honour your value, and to find hope whenever you look out onto the horizon. We all have a deep knowing within us, an inner voice helping us move through the world. Here is your invitation to free that voice.

The title, *Citrine Horizon,* was inspired by the one-of-a-kind Grand Canyon sunset I witnessed, the crystal, citrine, and my thyroid cancer scar. One of the meanings behind citrine is that it promotes thyroid health. Citrine's energy also helps you follow your true path. Its colour is the golden glow of the sunset or sunrise. Horizon in the title represents the beauty in my scar, which is also a straight horizontal line. The words citrine and horizon together connect my physical body to the enchanting Universe.

All medical professionals' identities have been altered for confidentiality. Experiences are all real, from my memory.

ACKNOWLEDGEMENTS

I WANT TO THANK MY PARENTS, Ted and Pam Seraphim, and my brother, Greg Seraphim. They navigated this difficult time so well and the love they shared held me up in the most challenging moments.

To the love of my life, Dustin Brooks—every morning I'm grateful to wake up to you. You are my hope and my light. Thank you for the boundless love and support you've given me through not only this time in my life but also while writing this book.

Ata Ojani, thank you for being my first friend on this earth. It is an honour to use your talent in creating the most exquisite cover art for *Citrine Horizon*.

To my first reader, Trish Sissons—I'm so fortunate to have received your insightful review to help strengthen my story. Thank you for always encouraging me since our university days.

To the rest of my dear family and friends, those mentioned in this story, and many who aren't but hold an equally special place in my heart—thank you for being there. For calling me, texting me, and sitting with me through moments I tried so hard to handle on my own. You knew your presence and love were needed.

My memories from my post-surgery days are hazy, but I know many people had me in their thoughts, sent cards, flowers, and gifts—I felt very loved. Thank you to everyone who was there for me in their own special way.

Thank you to my surgeon, who did an exceptional surgery removing all the cancer and giving me a now barely existent scar that expertly fits within the lines of my neck.

Thank you to my therapist for helping me access the tools within and introducing poetry as an outlet for my struggles.

Thank you to my astrologer and fellow Scorpio rising, Andrea Javor (Mystic Sandwich Astrology), for showing the potential of my humanity in the vast Universe. Thank you to my other spiritual teachers, Melanie Ptashynski (Just Breathe Reiki) and Bree Melanson, who tenderly guided me back to healing and trusting my soul.

Bon Iver/Justin Vernon, thank you for allowing me to use your lyrics from "Holocene." Your music has been with me through many defining moments in my life, and I'm grateful for your talent.

Thank you to my fabulous team at The Self Publishing Agency: Megan Williams, Kristy Twellmann Hill, Ira Vergani, et al. And special thank yous to my incredible editor, Tara McGuire, and magical storytelling coach, Anna Mullens. You both held my story so gently and coaxed me into unlocking difficult memories and valuable realizations. Working with both of you was gratifying and cathartic.

Most importantly, thank you to Dr. Tim Lepard. When I walked into your office at work that day, your sixth sense knew I needed to get an ultrasound on my neck, and I will forever be grateful to you.

THANKFUL

I'm thankful
for earth keeping me grounded
sky lifting me up
sun encouraging me to aim higher
moon fuelling my dreams

I'm thankful
for the way my partner
kisses me on the cheek in the morning
and my forehead at night
how his love surrounds me
and protects me to keep me soft
from the hard moments of this life

I'm thankful
for the morning greeting from my furry cats
and the good night pats before sleep
the moment of pause curling up
with the little furballs
that knead bread dough on my lap

I'm thankful
for breath practice
and body movement
for the food that delights
and nourishes me

I'm thankful
for the resilience and bravery
it takes to step out into this world
with love and hope and feeling

I'm thankful
for the close connections
of hands held and hugs given
the sharing of secrets and goals
and dreams

I'm thankful
for the moments where eye contact
says everything
for inside jokes
that make me chuckle
and companionship
that's loyal over everything

I'm thankful
for the birds
that sing in the morning
and that one nocturnal songbird
who sings lullabies as I sleep

I'm thankful
for the beauty and tragedy
of this life
for I am here to exist
to learn
to overcome
to grow
to be

ABOUT THE AUTHOR

HANNAH SERAPHIM is a writer, editor, and sound meditation practitioner. In 2019, Hannah quit her corporate job and took the leap of faith to reach her goal of setting foot on all seven continents, and to write about her thyroid cancer diagnosis at the age of twenty-six. She resides on the Coast Salish peoples' traditional, ancestral, and unceded territory–Squamish, Tsleil-Waututh, and Musqueam Nations, also known as North Vancouver, Canada, with her partner Dustin and cats Earl Grey and Lady Willow. *Citrine Horizon* is her first book. Visit the author's website at hannahseraphim.com.

Photo credit: Ata Ojani